FINDING CHRIST THROUGH THE BOOK OF MORMON

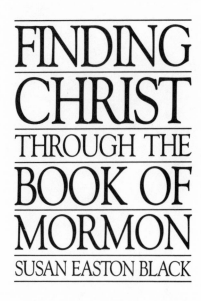

FINDING
CHRIST
THROUGH THE
BOOK OF
MORMON
SUSAN EASTON BLACK

Deseret Book Company
Salt Lake City, Utah

No part of this book may be reproduced in any
form or by any means without permission in writing
from the publisher, Deseret Book Company,
P.O. Box 30178, Salt Lake City, Utah 84130.
Deseret Book is a registered trademark of
Deseret Book Company.

First printing October 1987

Library of Congress Cataloging-in-Publication Data

Black, Susan Easton.
    Finding Christ through the Book of Mormon.

    Bibliography: p.
    Includes index.
    1. Jesus Christ—Mormon interpretations.   2. Book of
Mormon—Use.   I. Title.
BX8643.J4B53   1987   289.3'22   87-24318
ISBN 0-87579-099-2

Dedicated to
Brian, Todd, and John
with love and respect

CONTENTS

PREFACE

My purpose in writing this book is to share with you the answer I have found to the question, "Is the Book of Mormon another witness for Jesus Christ?" The words I write are sincere, born of years of prayerful searching that began so long ago. I hope they will convey to you the adventure of my quest, my unexpected discoveries along the way, and my subsequent joy in the knowledge that the Book of Mormon is indeed a powerful witness of Jesus Christ, our Savior and Redeemer.

I wish to share with you the highlights of what I have learned about the nature of our Heavenly Father and his son Jesus Christ. My hope is that these glimpses into eternal realms will benefit you in your own search to know God.

Chapter 1

THE CHALLENGE TO A FRAGILE TESTIMONY

*When ye shall read these things, if it
be wisdom in God that ye
should read them . . .*
Moroni 10:3

When I was ten years old, truly memorable adventures in the classroom were rare. Any dramatic variety in the daily routine of the school doldrums was to me a fresh breeze. That is why I anticipated what in the Long Beach School District was referred to as "religious released time": two weeks in which fifth- and sixth-grade students didn't attend school. Instead they attended a local church to study religion.

Excitedly I took home the note that informed my parents of my opportunity to be a part of "released time." When my father read the note and realized that my options were to attend either a Catholic cathedral, a Jewish synagogue, or a nondenominational church, he utterly refused to give his consent. I tried to console myself, but for two weeks while my friends attended religious education, I attended school alone. I vowed never again!

Running errands at home, clearing off the table, and cleaning my room all had the qualifying string attached: "Now will you let me attend 'released time'?" Month after month I reminded my father of the personal disaster school had been for me without my friends.

The night before "released time" was to occur in sixth

1

grade, my father finally gave in. At this point he included a few qualifiers of his own. I was to wear my green felt Primary bandlo and carry my Book of Mormon. In retrospect I can only suppose my father assumed that I would be fully clad in the armor of God and would be ready for any and all attacks to my testimony.

The attack did come that first day at religious education, from the minister of the nondenominational church. As he began to speak to the assembled children, he said that he would be talking about God, Christ, and the Holy Ghost. He explained to us, "They are three in one, and one in three."

Though perplexed by his statement, I listened intently to his explanation so that I could understand his message. His explanation did not define three in one or one in three but instead described where God lives. "Children, God is in a cloud."

I knew that God had a body, and so in my childish mind I began to see his body stretched until it was as large as a cloud. The Lord appeared huge to me.

With this image in my mind, I heard the minister say, "Children, God is in a tree."

I imagined this very large being now becoming elongated so that he could dwell in the trunk of a tree.

The minister further stated, "Children, God is in a flower."

In my mind the Lord had suddenly shrunk. He was very tiny.

I raised my hand. The minister droned on with a myriad of inconsistencies, and I started to wave my hand back and forth.

The minister's next statement that I remember hearing was "Children, God is in a raindrop."

In my mind I began to see rain dripping and said, "Are you in this drop? or in this one? or in that?"

I could stand this message no longer. I jumped to my feet and yelled, "Stop!"

The minister stopped. The boys and girls who had been whispering and passing notes stopped. The PTA mothers who were chaperoning us stopped their reprimanding. Everyone stopped and stared.

I said, "What you have just said is not true!"

"What is not true?" he asked.

I said boldly, "God does not live in a cloud, a tree trunk, a flower, or a raindrop. That is because God has a body just like mine and yours."

Visibly upset, the minister asked, "How do you know that?"

I quickly looked at my bandlo, hoping that it would give me a clue about where I had gotten my knowledge, but it did not. I looked at the book I was carrying. I then held up my large Book of Mormon and said, "It says so in this book."

"Oh that," replied the minister.

Dismissing the remainder of the opening devotional, he invited the other children to attend their religious education workshop classes for the day. He invited me to come immediately to his office.

I began to cry. My worried friends gathered around me. It was no small circle of friends that pointed the way to the minister's office. But alone I entered his room. He inquired about my bandlo, but he was definitely more interested in my book.

He asked, "Where in that book does it say God has a body?"

I flipped through quickly, hoping to open to just the right verse. He then exclaimed, "You appear to be having difficulty locating what you are seeking. Could it be that you have never read this book?"

With shame I admitted, "I have never read this book."

The result was that he told me to leave "released time" and return to school.

For the next two weeks I read the Book of Mormon. I cannot in all honesty say that during my first reading of the Book of Mormon I had an experience similar to that of Mary Elizabeth Rollins, who begged to read the book. Mary wrote, "I felt such a strong desire to read it, that I could not refrain from asking [Isaac Morley] to let me take it home and read it, while he attended meeting." (Lavina Fielding Anderson, "Kirtland's Resolute Saints," Ensign, Jan. 1979, p. 49.)

Nor was my experience equal to Parley P. Pratt's first reading of the book. Parley stated: "I read all day; eating was a burden, I had no desire for food; sleep was a burden when the night came, I preferred reading to sleep. As I read, the spirit of the Lord was upon me, and I knew and comprehended that the book was true, as plainly and manifestly as a man comprehends and knows that he exists. My joy was now full." [*Autobiography of Parley Parker Pratt*, pp. 36-37.]

Yet I can say that I read. I was looking intently for just the right answer to the question the minister had asked.

I was disappointed as I began my search not to find the answer in the first verse of 1 Nephi. As I read on, I learned about travels in the wilderness, broken bows, dreams, wickedness, and warfare—but where was my answer? I almost gave up as I struggled through the Isaiah chapters. As I read on and on, I found that the Book of Mormon contained many messages; yet my first reading of it left me in a quandary. Where was the answer I was seeking? I did not find it.

On reflection, I now view that first experience as comparable to that of a hurried tourist who exclaims, "Yes, I have been there. I saw the monuments, but I didn't get to know the people." In this case I said, "Of course I read the Book of Mormon, but I didn't find Christ." Not until several years and numerous rereadings later did I finally begin to discover how to read the Book of Mormon so that I could find the answer I had sought for so long.

That discovery occurred after a discussion I had with Robert J. Matthews, dean of Religious Education at Brigham Young University, on gaining a knowledge of my Father in Heaven, his son Jesus Christ, and the Holy Ghost. Dean Matthews said, "Susan, the best book for you to read to find the answer you seek is the Book of Mormon."

I was surprised at his suggestion and reminded him that I was teaching the Book of Mormon. I added that since childhood I had read and reread the book many times. It had long been my favorite.

He said, "I know that, Susan. This time I want you to read it and find Jesus. I want you to find him in each chapter. I want you to return with a testimony that the entire Book of Mormon is another witness for Jesus Christ."

That night, very discouraged and alone, I again opened the Book of Mormon and began reading the title page. One phrase caught my attention. I read it over and over again. Could Dean Matthews be right? Was this *entire* book about Christ? The phrase announced plainly and directly that the purpose of the book was "the convincing of the Jew and Gentile that Jesus is the Christ." If that was the purpose, then I had quite overlooked the book's recurrent, most powerful, most timely message. I had seen the surface and missed the heart.

I now know from years of diligent and prayerful searching that the Book of Mormon has been preserved to come forth in these latter days to convince the "Jew and Gentile that Jesus is the Christ, the Eternal God." Its purpose is to verify in thousands of references the divine sonship of Jesus to those who "ask with a sincere heart, with real intent, having faith in Christ." (Moroni 10:4.) I concur with Elder Bruce R. McConkie: "If ever there was a compilation of inspired writings that stand as a witness of the divine Sonship of the Lord Jesus Christ, that work is the Book of Mormon!" (*The Promised Messiah*, p. 145.)

CHRIST IS CENTRAL TO THE BOOK OF MORMON

By earnestly seeking, we can discover that the Book of Mormon writers wrote primarily about our Savior. They wrote of him because of their conviction of his divinity, for they knew him. Through the Holy Ghost these prophetic writers knew that their writings would bear testimony to a confused world that Jesus is the Christ and would help us to know him and love him.

He is so important to the Book of Mormon prophets that as they wrote their testimonies of the promised Messiah, they mentioned some form of his name on an average of every 1.7 verses. These prophetic scribes referred to Jesus Christ by, literally, 101 different names from the first reference to him as "Lord" in 1 Nephi 1:1 to the final name in the Book of Mormon given him as "Eternal Judge" in Moroni 10:34. Each of the 101 names signified to the prophets a different attribute or characteristic of him and was used appropriately to convey their recognition of who he is and what his mission represents. As a result, his profound character, his singular mission, and his divine relationship to us are most clearly revealed.

Not only did the ancient Book of Mormon prophets love to write Christ's name often but they particularly delighted to write about his earthly existence. It is apparent that their central message about his life in Jerusalem is the Atonement. Why is that event so significant? It is because "nothing in the entire plan of salvation compares in any way in importance with that most transcendent of all events." (Bruce R. McConkie, *Mormon Doctrine*, p. 60.)

Although many holy men living in the western hemisphere have known of, spoken of, and written of Christ, only a few of these righteous servants of God have recorded that they saw him. The exception to the few occurred in the Americas in A.D. 34. In that year, Jesus Christ visited the house of Joseph. A remnant of Joseph's seed saw, heard, and touched the resurrected Lord and recognized him as the Mediator, Redeemer, and the Chosen One of Israel. They tell us of Christ in ways that are unequaled.

The Book of Mormon contains the story of Christ's ministry to the western hemisphere. In that sacred text we learn of the dawning of a new dispensation of the gospel. We are privileged to witness through the written word the selection of twelve righteous men to be the Lord's disciples. We discover the healing power of Christ as we observe the lame, the blind, the withered, and all those who are afflicted made whole. This vivid, touching scene will grow even more tender for us as we vicariously watch the Holy One bless the assemblage of little children. We conclude that the multitude gathered around the temple in Bountiful in A.D. 34 were truly blessed. Nowhere in holy writ can we find a gathering of people that surpasses this one. Yet what they heard, what they saw, and what they felt as they witnessed the Savior and the ushering in of a new dispensation were only a prelude to the symphony that will be heard and seen and felt in the year of the Messiah's second coming.

The continual peace and harmony following the ascension of Jesus Christ was a marvelous reprieve from what was more commonly seen among the ancient inhabitants of America. Less than one-fourth of the writings of Nephite prophets speaks of the positive effects that occur when people follow the teachings of Christ. Most of the Nephite record is dominated by war, famine, and destruction because most of the time the people chose to reject our Savior and his teachings.

By analyzing the nature of Christ as set forth in the Book of Mormon, we can understand the significance of this wrong choice. The Lord is a living God who possesses a body with parts and with passions. References to God's having body parts occur 283 times in the Book of Mormon. The Lord showed us that his body was used to assist and benefit the people. For example, he symbolically used his hands to guide (2 Nephi 1:24) and to recover (2 Nephi 21:11) his children. References to God's having passions are recorded in 320 verses. The deep emotions involving the Lord's attributes of love are recorded 211 times, while the judgmental passions of God are recorded 99 times. This enumeration illustrates that the Lord showed forth doubly (two to one) his passions of love.

This ratio is especially significant when we realize that Christ showed forth great loving passions even though his people chose to reject him. They did not reject him in ignorance, because the Lord had not left his people in darkness about his will and teachings; rather, the burden of responsibility was on the people, because they had been taught the gospel and then chose to disobey.

The recurring theme of the flat rejection of the word of God by most ancient Americans may lead us to conclude that the Book of Mormon is little more than a methodical course for spiritual failure. That conclusion would be incorrect. The Book of Mormon not only clearly defines a path for spiritual and material ruin but also presents the narrow path that leads to spiritual well-being.

A few faithful followers found the narrow path and in their actions emulated the life of Christ. They sought to declare the word of God. (Mosiah 3:3.) Through the words of God they brought peace to a war-torn land. (Words of Mormon 1:18.) They exhorted the majority to be faithful and to repent of their sins. (Helaman 6:4.) They testified boldly concerning the redemption of the Lord. (3 Nephi 6:20.)

As a result, they endured suffering and persecution for their beliefs. Amid the extreme mocking, anger, gnashing of teeth, and other persecution, one truth is poignantly clear:

the Lord will not leave his devoted followers comfortless. In affliction, persecution, and suffering the Lord sends heavenly aid.

In the Book of Mormon we discover that sorrow eventually becomes glory. Persecution proves a crown for the righteous. Heavenly strength does come to those worthy faithful followers who do not fear persecution but who seek to do the will of God and to keep his commandments. (Helaman 10:4–10.) We learn that their consistent faithfulness, devotion, and willingness to submit to all things earned for an elect few the assurance of eternal life.

As each man, woman, and child who inhabited ancient America chose to accept or reject Christ, so must we, too. Is he our Savior? Did he pass through the agony of Gethsemane and give his life so that we might live? Will he yet come in glory as the Prince of Peace, the King of Heaven and Earth?

This one choice is not the only one that we must make on the Saturday eve before the coming of the Savior in his majesty. If we concur that Jesus is the Christ and that we have learned much of him and his teachings from studying the Book of Mormon, yet one more issue needs to be addressed. That issue is, Who is Joseph Smith? Was he prophet, seer, revelator, and translator? The Book of Mormon is a witness that Jesus is the Christ and a testimony that Joseph Smith was raised up to translate this "marvellous work and a wonder." (Isaiah 29:14.)

A TESTIMONY OF JOSEPH, A WITNESS OF CHRIST

To write of the glorious message of the Book of Mormon without writing of the divine calling of its translator is impossible. The very existence of this holy scripture proclaims that Joseph Smith was a prophet, a seer, a revelator, and, yes, a translator.

The contents of this book are an irrefutable testament that Jesus is the Son of God. Christ is the central focus of the Book of Mormon. The reason for the focus on Christ is that the Book of Mormon was preserved to come forth in these latter days to convince a confused generation, "Jew and Gentile," through its contents "that Jesus is the Christ, the Eternal God." (Title page.)

The Savior has testified, eleven witnesses have testified, and the prophets of The Church of Jesus Christ of Latter-day Saints have testified of the truthfulness of the Book of Mormon. Each knew that metal plates and interpreters had been preserved to come forth in the latter days to our generation. Each knew that this "marvellous work and a wonder" was translated by the Prophet Joseph Smith.

After all the testimonies that have been written and spoken of the Book of Mormon, the key question remains, What do you think of the book? If the book is what it claims to be, if the original record was written on plates of metal and revealed by a holy angel to Joseph, if the translation was made by the power of God, then each of us has the right to know that it is true. It is my humble testimony that the Book of Mormon is the word of God. It is a second witness that Jesus is the Christ. Its very existence proclaims that Joseph Smith was a prophet and a translator. That is what I profess. That is what I know.

Chapter 2

TO THE CONVINCING OF THE JEW AND GENTILE THAT JESUS IS THE CHRIST

*When ye shall read these
things, . . . remember how merciful
the Lord hath been.
Moroni 10:3*

Since 1830 the critic, the scholar, the curious, and even the well-meaning have all tried to explain the Book of Mormon, but in so doing they have paid little attention to its announced central message, Jesus Christ. In the preface to the book, Moroni clearly affirmed that its purpose centers in Christ.

Hostile critics have certainly passed by Moroni's preface, for they dismiss the Book of Mormon as a hoax and a fraud, evidence of Joseph Smith's imagination. Their condemnation of this holy scripture on the basis of their purported research, exclusive information, and assumed expertise about the origin of the book is riddled with intellectual caverns. The critics' ill-founded attacks warrant no scholarly credence. When they hurl their gratuitous verbiage at the word of God, they, not the book, appear foolish. And not so amazingly, they never discover that the Book of Mormon is centered in Christ.

Many sympathetic archaeologists, interested in external evidence, suggest that their purpose in perusing the Book of

Mormon is to explore hypotheses regarding archaeological artifacts in the Americas, not to be convinced that Jesus is the Christ. Many discoveries in recent years by American archaeologists have overturned the assurances of earlier scholars that the Book of Mormon contradicts archaeological evidence.

Archaeologists have verified the assurance of the Book of Mormon that there were in pre-Columbian America complex monetary systems (Alma 11:4–19), cement (Helaman 3:7, 9, 11), copper (1 Nephi 18:25; 2 Nephi 5:15), sophisticated tools (1 Nephi 17.9; Jarom 1:8; Ether 10:25–26), machinery (Jarom 1:8), and excellent highways (3 Nephi 6:8). Scholars have found evidence of advanced civilizations, fluctuations in economic growth, trends in migration, and devastations of war—centuries after Book of Mormon prophets recorded these events. Museums throughout North and South America now support many of the historical references of the Book of Mormon and bolster scholars' hypotheses. But as interesting and eventually consistent as these findings are with the cultural details of the Book of Mormon, these scholars, too, have rarely gone beyond the details to discover the living core: the myriad of revelations of Jesus the Christ.

Other scholars, comparative anthropologists, focusing on ancient Old World culture and worship, see the Book of Mormon as a point of reference for comparing and contrasting eastern and western civilizations. For example, both cultures wrote on plates of metal (1 Nephi 4:16), regarded oaths as binding (1 Nephi 4:33, 35, 37), held sacred the law of Moses (using burnt offerings in worship; 1 Nephi 5:9; 7:22; Mosiah 2:3), intermixed idol worship in their culture (Helaman 6:31; Alma 17:15; 31:1), had apostates who made sacrifices to idols (Mormon 4:14, 21), and built altars of stones (1 Nephi 2:7; Alma 17:4). These similarities, along with curious but explainable differences, are intellectually stimulating but not always spiritually edifying. Such scholarship also often misses the Christ-centered purpose of the book.

To the merely curious, one major point in the Book of Mormon is the account of a white god visiting the people of the western hemisphere. The Book of Mormon calls this white god Christ. The people of Mexico call their white, bearded god *Quetzalcoatl;* the Polynesian cultures call theirs *Wakea;* the primitive Indian tribes on the upper Amazon River in South America refer to him as *Wako;* and the Indians in the Andean Region call him *Viracocha.* These legends strengthen the idea of an actual visit of Deity to America, but how convincing is this evidence? The curious person must look beneath these interesting surface details to discover the revealed Christ.

Indeed, the Book of Mormon is much more than a history of the adventures of the people who inhabited the western hemisphere from about 590 B.C. to A.D. 421. As the pages of the text unfold, we learn of civilizations plagued by evil men and women: robbers (Helaman 2), anti-Christs (Alma 30), and seductresses (Alma 39). We learn of treachery (Alma 47), wars (Alma 43; Helaman 4), defense tactics (Alma 43), and prison walls (Helaman 5:27). By contrast, we also learn of courageous kings (Mosiah 2; 27), of integrity (Mosiah 11–17), and of faithfulness (Alma 32). The plot of the Book of Mormon is high adventure in the great contest between the forces of good and evil. These combine to present, even to the first-time reader, a vibrant, intriguing history of a people oscillating between grandeur and destruction.

Christ is the central theme on every page of the Book of Mormon. His reality has inspired thousands of faithful Latter-day Saint missionaries who since 1830 have spent millions of dollars to travel the globe, sharing the Book of Mormon. They have certainly not labored merely to share a book of high adventure, a treatise on archaeological ruins, a manuscript on the origin of some American Indians, or a comparative study of Indian legends. The people in Germany, South Africa, Korea, England, or Australia would probably have little interest in acquiring such a text and reading it if mere historical fact were its purpose.

It is not. Christ is the central purpose. Is it conceivable that a mere history translated from reformed Egyptian into English in 1830 would still be in print by 1987? By 1986, the Book of Mormon was not only in print in the English language but had been translated into thirty-six languages, and portions of the book had been translated into thirty-four other languages. A conservative count indicates that in English alone 1,693,151 copies of the Book of Mormon were distributed in the year 1986. (Personal telephone conversation with Rick Crowther of The Church of Jesus Christ of Latter-day Saints Distribution Center, Salt Lake City, Utah, July 17, 1986.)

The reason for this compelling effect worldwide is the revelation of Christ, not the background details in the Book of Mormon that have fascinated some. Perhaps a few polite or interested scholars or the curious might agree to read the book for superficial reasons, but only a promise of deeply significant effects would induce the majority to read it. In our fast-paced, twentieth-century lives, most individuals would not be inclined to read a double-columned book of over five hundred pages if it were presented merely as something of interest to the scholar, the curious, or the well-meaning. If we were to recognize, however, that through pondering its message we could comprehend, as we could in no other way, the nature of our Father in Heaven, his son Jesus the Christ, and the Holy Ghost, we would understand why so many continue to read the Book of Mormon with intensity.

Unfortunately, many readers settle for something far less than finding Christ in the Book of Mormon. Failing to find the key, they fail to recognize the reason that has moved missionaries, pioneers, and Latter-day Saints to devote all to the quest. These Saints have discovered that the Book of Mormon is an amazingly rich and powerful witness of Jesus Christ. It witnesses not only that he is but also who he is, how he thinks, how he feels, and how he acts. The richness of what is revealed about Jesus Christ unfolds as we begin to know of the Godhead, and especially of Jesus the Christ, through the Book of Mormon. We gradually enter into its holy inner meanings after merely admiring the surrounding courtyards. We come to truly know of Jesus the Christ through the catalytic words of the Book of Mormon prophets, for their central purpose was to reveal him to us. Beginning with chapter 1 of 1 Nephi, the first chapter of the Book of Mormon, we learn that—

1. The Lord highly favored Nephi in all his days. (1 Nephi 1:1.)

2. Knowledge of the goodness and mysteries of God is available to us. (1 Nephi 1:1.)

3. The way to speak to the Lord is through prayer. (1 Nephi 1:5.)

4. We can receive heavenly manifestations while praying to the Lord with all our heart. (1 Nephi 1:6.)

5. God is seen in vision sitting on a throne surrounded by angels singing and praising him. (1 Nephi 1:8.)

6. The Lord can show future events to us. (1 Nephi 1:9–13, 15.)

7. We can be filled with the Spirit of the Lord. (1 Nephi 1:12.)

8. The correct response to a heavenly manifestation is to praise God: "Great and marvelous are thy works, O Lord God Almighty!" (1 Nephi 1:14.)

9. The Messiah will come to redeem the world. (1 Nephi 1:19.)

10. The Lord is merciful to "those whom he hath chosen, because of their faith, to make them mighty even unto the power of deliverance." (1 Nephi 1:20.)

The information available to those who truly wish to know and to be like Christ far supersedes in importance the almost irrelevant but prevalent discussions of whether the bow that Nephi broke was made of pure steel or a combination of wood and steel (1 Nephi 16:18); or why Lehi wanted Lemuel to be firm and steadfast as a valley instead of firm and steadfast as a mountain or a rock (1 Nephi 2:10); or whether Noah's ark was really shaped like the Jaredite barges (Ether 6:7). Answers to these questions might add an awareness of the background of the text, but they do not lead us directly to the central message, the convincing assurance that "Jesus is the Christ, the Eternal God." (Title page of the Book of Mormon.)

If we seek to know, we will find that the Book of Mormon writers wrote primarily about our Savior. They wrote of him because of their conviction of his divinity, for they knew of him and loved him: "For, for this intent have we written these things, that they may know that we knew of Christ, and we had a hope of his glory many hundred years before his coming; and not only we ourselves had a hope of his glory, but also all the holy prophets which were before us." (Jacob 4:4.)

They did not gain this knowledge of Christ through a comparison of the customs, characteristics, life-styles, and mannerisms of Lehi's family with those of peoples living around the land of Jerusalem in 600 B.C. Nor did they gain knowledge of Jesus through findings unearthed by archaeologists, such as skeletal remains, gold plates, cement highways, and places of worship in the Americas. Neither did they grasp a knowledge of the Messiah through acquaintance with Indian traditions, folklore, or legends of voyages and wars. The Holy One was revealed to the ancient prophets of the Book of Mormon by the power of the Holy Ghost. By the power of the Holy Ghost, these prophets wrote a second witness for Jesus Christ—the Book of Mormon—and by that same power, the ancient prophets knew that their writings would bear testimony to us that Jesus is the Christ. If we do not seek it, we can almost completely miss that testimony. If we do seek it, it reverberates, dominates, and thunders on every page, in every chapter, in every verse, and in nearly every sentence!

The Book of Mormon prophets mentioned some form of Christ's name on an average of once every 1.7 verses. By comparison, the New Testament writers mentioned a form of his name on an average of once every 2.1 verses. (Lee A. Crandall, *New Testament Study on the Use of the Names of Deity*, n.p.) Thus, the name of the Savior appears nearly 25 percent more frequently in the Book of Mormon than even in the New Testament. When we realize that a verse usually consists of one sentence, it appears that we cannot, on the average, read two sentences in the Book of Mormon without seeing some form of Christ's name.

These references to Christ are not distributed without appropriate relationship to the text. For instance, fewer references to Christ are made during periods of darkness, apostasy, and war, probably because his influence is lessened by the unrighteous actions of the people. (See, for example, Alma 50–59.) During periods of peace, joy, and prosperity, which come when the people keep the commandments, the names of the Son of Righteousness are used profusely, because circumstances indicate the abundant presence of his spirit. (See, for example, 4 Nephi.)

Books	References to Christ	Verses	Number of verses per appearance of Christ's name
1 Nephi	474	618	1.303
2 Nephi	591	779	1.318
Jacob	156	203	1.301
Enos	22	27	1.227
Jarom	8	15	1.875
Omni	20	30	1.500
Words of Mormon	15	18	1.200
Mosiah	492	785	1.596
Alma	1,013	1,975	1.950
Helaman	225	497	2.209
3 Nephi	293	788	2.689
4 Nephi	42	49	1.167
Mormon	188	227	1.207
Ether	220	433	1.968
Moroni	166	163	1.018
TOTALS	3,925	6,607	1.7

Seeking for Christ in the Book of Mormon reveals unexpected treasure. His name appears often throughout the
entire book, but it does not appear as a monotonous or
chanting repetition. Each appearance of his name reveals
something unique, something essential, and something
deeply inspirational about him. By tallying how many different names designate Christ, we discover that the prophetic scribes of the Book of Mormon referred to Jesus Christ
by, literally, 101 different names. Here listed alphabetically
are those names for the Son of God:

Almighty (2 Nephi 23:6)
Almighty God (Jacob 2:10)
Alpha and Omega (3 Nephi 9:18)
Being (Mosiah 4:19)
Beloved (2 Nephi 31:15)
Beloved Son (2 Nephi 31:11)
Christ (2 Nephi 10:3)
Christ Jesus (Alma 5:44)
Christ the Son (Alma 11:44)
Counselor (2 Nephi 19:6)
Creator (2 Nephi 9:5)
Eternal Father (Mosiah 15:4)
Eternal God (1 Nephi 12:18)

Eternal Head (Helaman 13:38)
Eternal Judge (Moroni 10:34)
Everlasting Father (2 Nephi 19:6)
Everlasting God (1 Nephi 15:15)
Father (Jacob 7:22)
Father of heaven (1 Nephi 22:9)
Father of heaven and of earth (Helaman 14:12)
Founder of peace (Mosiah 15:18)
God (2 Nephi 1:22)
God of Abraham (1 Nephi 19:10)
God of Abraham, and Isaac, and Jacob (Mosiah 7:19)
God of Abraham, and of Isaac, and the God of Jacob (1 Nephi 19:10)
God of Isaac (Alma 29:11)
God of Israel (1 Nephi 19:7)
God of Jacob (2 Nephi 12:3)
God of miracles (2 Nephi 27:23)
God of nature (1 Nephi 19:12)
God of the whole earth (3 Nephi 11:14)
Good shepherd (Alma 5:38)
Great Creator (2 Nephi 9:5)
Great Spirit (Alma 18:2)
Head (Jacob 4:17)
Holy Child (Moroni 8:3)
Holy God (2 Nephi 9:39)
Holy Messiah (2 Nephi 2:6)
Holy One (2 Nephi 2:10)
Holy One of Israel (1 Nephi 19:14)
Holy One of Jacob (2 Nephi 27:34)
Husband (3 Nephi 22:5)
Immanuel (2 Nephi 18:8)
Jehovah (Moroni 10:34)
Jesus (2 Nephi 31:10)
Jesus Christ (2 Nephi 25:19)
Keeper of the gate (2 Nephi 9:41)
King (2 Nephi 16:5)
King of heaven (2 Nephi 10:14)
Lamb (1 Nephi 13:35)
Lamb of God (1 Nephi 10:10)
Lord (1 Nephi 10:14)
Lord God (2 Nephi 1:5)
Lord God Almighty (2 Nephi 9:46)
Lord God Omnipotent (Mosiah 3:21)
Lord God of Hosts (2 Nephi 13:15)
Lord Jehovah (2 Nephi 22:2)
Lord Jesus (Moroni 6:6)
Lord Jesus Christ (Mosiah 3:12)

Lord of Hosts (1 Nephi 20:2)
Lord of the vineyard (Jacob 5:8)
Lord Omnipotent (Mosiah 3:5)
Maker (2 Nephi 9:40)
Man (3 Nephi 11:8)
Master (Jacob 5:4)
Mediator (2 Nephi 2:28)
Messiah (1 Nephi 1:19)
Mighty God (2 Nephi 6:17)
Mighty One of Israel (1 Nephi 22:12)
Mighty One of Jacob (1 Nephi 21:26)
Most High (2 Nephi 24:14)
Most High God (Alma 26:14)
Only Begotten of the Father (2 Nephi 25:12)
Only Begotten Son (Jacob 4:5)
Prince of Peace (2 Nephi 19:6)
Prophet (1 Nephi 22:20)
Rabbanah (Alma 18:13)
Redeemer (1 Nephi 10:6)
Redeemer of Israel (1 Nephi 21:7)
Redeemer of the world (1 Nephi 10:5)
Rock (1 Nephi 15:15)
Savior (2 Nephi 31:13)
Savior Jesus Christ (3 Nephi 5:20)
Savior of the world (1 Nephi 10:4)
Shepherd (1 Nephi 13:41)
Son (2 Nephi 31:13)
Son of God (1 Nephi 10:17)
Son of Righteousness (Ether 9:22)
Son of the Eternal Father (1 Nephi 11:21)
Son of the everlasting God (1 Nephi 11:32)
Son of the living God (2 Nephi 31:16)
Son of the most high God (1 Nephi 11:6)
Stone (Jacob 4:16)
Supreme Being (Alma 11:22)
Supreme Creator (Alma 30:44)
True and living God (1 Nephi 17:30)
True Messiah (2 Nephi 1:10)
True shepherd (Helaman 15:13)
True vine (1 Nephi 15:15)
Well Beloved (Helaman 5:47)
Wonderful (2 Nephi 19:6)

The following table shows the number of times the various names for Christ occur in each book in the Book of Mormon:

Name / Specific verse	1 Nephi	2 Nephi	Jacob	Enos	Jarom	Omni	Words of Mormon	Mosiah	Alma	Helaman	3 Nephi	4 Nephi	Mormon	Ether	Moroni	Total	Percent
Almighty — *2 Nephi 23:6*	0	1	0	0	0	0	0	0	0	1	0	0	0	0	0	2	0
Almighty God — *Jacob 2:10*	1	0	1	0	0	0	0	2	0	0	0	0	0	0	0	4	0
Alpha and Omega — *3 Nephi 9:18*	0	0	0	0	0	0	0	0	0	0	1	0	0	0	0	1	0
Being — *Mosiah 4:19*	0	0	0	0	0	0	0	1	1	0	0	0	3	0	0	5	0
Beloved — *2 Nephi 31:15*	0	1	0	0	0	0	0	0	0	0	0	0	1	0	0	2	0
Beloved Son — *2 Nephi 31:11*	0	1	0	0	0	0	0	0	0	0	2	0	0	0	0	3	0
Christ — *2 Nephi 10:3*	0	49	26	3	0	1	5	27	65	9	22	15	20	8	62	312	8
Christ Jesus — *Alma 5:44*	0	0	0	0	0	0	0	0	1	0	0	0	0	0	0	1	0
Christ the Son — *Alma 11:44*	0	0	0	0	0	0	0	0	1	0	0	0	0	0	0	1	0
Counselor — *2 Nephi 19:6*	0	1	0	0	0	0	0	0	0	0	0	0	0	0	0	1	0

Name / Specific verse	1 Nephi	2 Nephi	Jacob	Enos	Jarom	Omni	Words of Mormon	Mosiah	Alma	Helaman	3 Nephi	4 Nephi	Mormon	Ether	Moroni	Total	Percent
Creator *2 Nephi 9:5*	0	0	2	0	0	1	0	2	1	1	0	0	0	0	0	7	0
Eternal Father *Mosiah 15:4*	0	0	0	0	0	0	0	0	2	0	0	0	1	0	1	4	0
Eternal God *1 Nephi 12:18*	1	2	0	0	0	0	0	0	2	0	0	0	0	1	0	6	0
Eternal Head *Helaman 13:38*	0	0	0	0	0	0	0	0	0	1	0	0	0	0	0	1	0
Eternal Judge *Moroni 10:34*	0	0	0	0	0	0	0	0	0	0	0	0	0	0	1	1	0
Everlasting Father *2 Nephi 19:6*	0	1	0	0	0	0	0	2	0	0	0	0	0	0	0	3	0
Everlasting God *1 Nephi 15:15*	1	1	0	0	0	0	0	0	0	0	0	0	0	0	0	2	0
Father *Jacob 7:22*	2	0	1	0	0	0	0	8	0	1	5	0	2	8	4	31	1
Father of heaven *1 Nephi 22:9*	1	0	0	0	0	0	0	0	0	0	0	0	0	0	0	1	0
Father of heaven and of earth *Helaman 14:12*	0	1	0	0	0	0	0	0	0	1	0	0	0	0	0	2	0

Entry	1	2	3	4	5	6	7	8	9	10	11	12	13	14	15	16	17
Founder of peace *Mosiah 15:18*	0	1	0	0	0	0	0	0	0	1	0	0	0	0	0	0	0
God *2 Nephi 1:22*	34	1351	46	31	52	8	49	78	564	221	7	3	2	8	48	139	95
God of Abraham *1 Nephi 19:10*	0	5	0	0	1	0	1	0	2	0	0	0	0	0	0	0	1
God of Abraham, and Isaac, and Jacob *Mosiah 7:19*	0	2	0	0	0	0	0	0	0	2	0	0	0	0	0	0	0
God of Abraham, and of Isaac, and the God of Jacob *1 Nephi 19:10*	0	1	0	0	0	0	0	0	0	0	0	0	0	0	0	0	1
God of Isaac *Alma 29:11*	0	5	0	0	1	0	1	0	2	0	0	0	0	0	0	0	1
God of Israel *1 Nephi 19:7*	0	11	0	0	0	0	2	0	0	0	0	0	0	0	0	2	7
God of Jacob *2 Nephi 12:3*	0	6	0	0	1	0	1	0	2	0	0	0	0	0	0	1	1
God of miracles *2 Nephi 27:23*	0	1	0	0	0	0	0	0	0	0	0	0	0	0	0	1	0
God of nature *1 Nephi 19:12*	0	1	0	0	0	0	0	0	0	0	0	0	0	0	0	0	1
God of the whole earth *3 Nephi 11:14*	0	2	0	0	0	0	2	0	0	0	0	0	0	0	0	0	0
Good shepherd *Alma 5:38*	0	8	0	0	0	0	0	1	7	0	0	0	0	0	0	0	0

Name / Specific verse	1 Nephi	2 Nephi	Jacob	Enos	Jarom	Omni	Words of Mormon	Mosiah	Alma	Helaman	3 Nephi	4 Nephi	Mormon	Ether	Moroni	Total	Percent
Great Creator *2 Nephi 9:5*	0	2	0	0	0	0	0	0	0	0	0	0	0	0	0	2	0
Great Spirit *Alma 18:2*	0	0	0	0	0	0	0	0	18	0	0	0	0	0	0	18	0
Head *Jacob 4:17*	0	0	1	0	0	0	0	2	0	0	0	0	0	0	0	3	0
Holy Child *Moroni 8:3*	0	0	0	0	0	0	0	0	0	0	0	0	0	0	1	1	0
Holy God *2 Nephi 9:39*	0	1	0	0	0	0	0	0	1	0	0	0	0	0	0	2	0
Holy Messiah *2 Nephi 2:6*	0	2	0	0	0	0	0	0	0	0	0	0	0	0	0	2	0
Holy One *2 Nephi 2:10*	1	3	0	0	0	0	0	0	2	1	0	0	1	0	0	8	0
Holy One of Israel *1 Nephi 19:14*	9	28	0	0	0	2	0	0	0	0	1	0	0	0	0	40	1
Holy One of Jacob *2 Nephi 27:34*	0	1	0	0	0	0	0	0	0	0	0	0	0	0	0	1	0
Husband *3 Nephi 22:5*	0	0	0	0	0	0	0	0	0	0	1	0	0	0	0	1	0

Title (Reference)																	
Immanuel — 2 Nephi 18:8	0	2	0	0	0	0	0	0	0	0	0	0	0	0	0	2	0
Jehovah — Moroni 10:34	0	0	0	0	0	0	0	0	0	0	0	0	0	0	1	1	0
Jesus — 2 Nephi 31:10	0	5	1	0	0	0	0	0	2	0	75	11	11	6	2	113	3
Jesus Christ — 2 Nephi 25:19	0	4	0	0	0	0	0	3	8	3	11	0	11	5	6	51	1
Keeper of the gate — 2 Nephi 9:41	0	1	0	0	0	0	0	0	0	0	0	0	0	0	0	1	0
King — 2 Nephi 16:5	0	1	0	0	0	0	0	1	2	0	0	0	0	0	0	4	0
King of heaven — 2 Nephi 10:14	0	1	0	0	0	0	0	0	0	0	0	0	0	0	0	1	0
Lamb — 1 Nephi 13:35	28	0	0	0	0	0	0	0	2	1	0	0	1	2	0	34	1
Lamb of God — 1 Nephi 10:10	28	4	0	0	0	0	0	0	1	0	0	0	2	0	0	35	1
Lord — 1 Nephi 10:14	232	191	19	7	5	13	3	189	253	103	81	8	70	148	28	1350	34
Lord God — 2 Nephi 1:5	11	53	6	2	0	0	0	8	15	3	0	0	0	4	2	104	3
Lord God Almighty — 2 Nephi 9:46	1	2	0	0	0	0	0	0	0	0	1	0	0	0	0	4	0
Lord God Omnipotent — Mosiah 3:21	0	0	0	0	0	0	0	1	0	0	0	0	0	0	0	1	0

Name / Specific verse	1 Nehi	2 Nephi	Jacob	Enos	Jarom	Omni	Words of Mormon	Mosiah	Alma	Helaman	3 Nephi	4 Nephi	Mormon	Ether	Moroni	Total	Percent
Lord God of Hosts *2 Nephi 13:15*	0	5	0	0	0	0	0	0	0	0	0	0	0	0	0	5	0
Lord Jehovah *2 Nephi 22:2*	0	1	0	0	0	0	0	0	0	0	0	0	0	0	0	1	0
Lord Jesus *Moroni 6:6*	0	0	0	0	0	0	0	0	0	0	0	0	0	1	1	2	0
Lord Jesus Christ *Mosiah 3:12*	0	0	0	0	0	0	0	1	4	1	3	0	1	1	3	14	0
Lord of Hosts *1 Nephi 20:2*	2	30	6	0	0	0	0	0	0	3	11	0	0	0	0	52	1
Lord of the vineyard *Jacob 5:8*	0	0	33	0	0	0	0	0	0	0	0	0	0	0	0	33	1
Lord Omnipotent *Mosiah 3:5*	0	0	0	0	0	0	0	5	0	0	0	0	0	0	0	5	0
Maker *2 Nephi 9:40*	0	1	1	1	0	0	0	0	0	1	1	0	0	0	0	5	0
Man *3 Nephi 11:8*	0	0	0	0	0	0	0	0	0	0	1	0	0	0	0	1	0
Master *Jacob 5:4*	0	0	6	0	0	0	0	1	0	0	0	0	0	0	0	7	0

Mediator *2 Nephi 2:28*	0	1	0	0	0	0	0	0	0	0	0	0	1	0
Messiah *1 Nephi 1:19*	1	28	0	0	0	0	1	0	0	0	0	1	13	12
Mighty God *2 Nephi 6:17*	0	3	0	0	0	0	0	0	0	0	0	0	3	0
Mighty One of Israel *1 Nephi 22:12*	0	1	0	0	0	0	0	0	0	0	0	0	0	1
Mighty One of Jacob *1 Nephi 21:26*	0	2	0	0	0	0	0	0	0	0	0	0	1	1
Most High *2 Nephi 24:14*	0	1	0	0	0	0	0	0	0	0	0	0	1	0
Most High God *Alma 26:14*	0	5	0	0	3	0	1	0	0	0	0	0	0	1
Only Begotten of the Father *2 Nephi 25:12*	0	4	0	0	0	0	3	0	0	0	0	1	0	0
Only Begotten Son *Jacob 4:5*	0	5	0	0	0	0	3	0	0	0	0	2	0	0
Prince of Peace *2 Nephi 19:6*	0	1	0	0	0	0	0	0	0	0	0	0	1	0
Prophet *1 Nephi 22:20*	0	6	0	0	1	0	0	0	0	0	0	0	0	5
Rabbanah *Alma 18:13*	0	2	0	0	0	0	2	0	0	0	0	0	0	0
Redeemer *1 Nephi 10:6*	1	37	1	0	5	3	6	4	0	0	0	1	8	9

Name	Specific verse	1 Nephi	2 Nephi	Jacob	Enos	Jarom	Omni	Words of Mormon	Mosiah	Alma	Helaman	3 Nephi	4 Nephi	Mormon	Ether	Moroni	Total	Percent
Redeemer of Israel	1 Nephi 21:7	1	0	0	0	0	0	0	0	0	0	0	0	0	0	0	1	0
Redeemer of the world	1 Nephi 10:5	2	0	0	0	0	0	0	0	0	0	0	0	0	0	0	2	0
Rock	1 Nephi 15:15	1	5	1	0	0	0	0	0	0	0	0	0	0	0	0	7	0
Savior	2 Nephi 31:13	2	2	0	0	0	0	0	1	0	0	0	0	2	0	1	8	0
Savior Jesus Christ	3 Nephi 5:20	0	0	0	0	0	0	0	0	0	0	1	0	1	0	0	2	0
Savior of the world	1 Nephi 10:4	2	0	0	0	0	0	0	0	0	0	0	0	0	0	0	2	0
Shepherd	1 Nephi 13:41	1	0	0	0	0	0	0	0	0	0	0	0	0	0	0	1	0
Son	2 Nephi 31:13	0	7	0	0	0	0	0	6	15	1	4	0	2	3	6	44	1
Son of God	1 Nephi 10:17	5	2	0	0	0	0	0	3	23	9	5	0	2	2	0	51	1
Son of Righteousness	Ether 9:22	0	1	0	0	0	0	0	0	0	0	1	0	0	1	0	3	0

Son of the Eternal Father *1 Nephi 11:21*	2	0	0	0	0	0	0	0	0	0	0	0	0	0	2	0
Son of the everlasting God *1 Nephi 11:32*	1	0	0	0	0	0	0	0	0	0	0	0	0	0	1	0
Son of the living God *2 Nephi 31:16*	0	1	0	0	0	0	0	0	0	1	0	0	2	0	4	0
Son of the most high God *1 Nephi 11:6*	1	0	0	0	0	0	0	0	0	0	0	0	0	0	1	0
Stone *Jacob 4:16*	0	0	2	0	0	0	0	0	0	0	0	0	0	0	2	0
Supreme Being *Alma 11:22*	0	0	0	0	0	0	0	0	1	0	0	0	0	0	1	0
Supreme Creator *Alma 30:44*	0	0	0	0	0	0	0	0	1	0	0	0	0	0	1	0
True and living God *1 Nephi 17:30*	1	0	0	0	0	0	0	0	0	0	0	0	0	0	1	0
True Messiah *2 Nephi 1:10*	0	2	0	0	0	0	0	0	0	0	0	0	0	0	2	0
True shepherd *Helaman 15:13*	0	0	0	0	0	0	0	0	0	1	0	0	0	0	1	0
True vine *1 Nephi 15:15*	1	0	0	0	0	0	0	0	0	0	0	0	0	0	1	0
Well Beloved *Helaman 5:47*	0	2	0	0	0	0	0	0	0	1	0	0	0	0	3	0
Wonderful *2 Nephi 19:6*	0	1	0	0	0	0	0	0	0	0	0	0	0	0	1	0
TOTALS	474	591	156	22	8	20	15	492	1013	225	293	42	188	220	166	3925

It is not surprising that the titles by which Christ is known have no negative connotations. On the other hand, the prophets, with repeated emphasis, called people in their generation by negative titles, for example, adulterers (2 Nephi 2:23), prideful (Jacob 2:13), and damned (Mormon 2:13). Reserved consistently for the Savior of mankind are the revered, positive titles, because negative characteristics and traits do not exist in the Holy One.

Each of the 101 names signified to the prophetic writers a different attribute or characteristic of our God, and each name was used to convey recognition of who he is and what his mission represents. For example, Lord Omnipotent means that Christ is the Lord of all, possessing all power. Holy One signifies that he is holy and without sin, being perfect in all things. God of the whole earth reflects his universal interest in all people and in their individual redemption. And Savior means that Jesus came to save his people from their sins.

The names given to our Lord take on new significance when we approach them through a thoughtful and a sensitive study of their meanings. Each title signifying Christ is in correct contextual usage each time it appears. His character and mission and his divine relationship to us are thereby more clearly revealed. Each verse is given enriched meaning because of the definition of Christ's name.

The following list of names for Christ and their meanings was drawn from *Mormon Doctrine*, by Elder Bruce R. McConkie.

Almighty God. This title signifies a holy being having all power and unlimited might.

Alpha and Omega. These words, being the first and last letters of the Greek alphabet, are used figuratively to teach the timelessness and eternal nature of our Lord's existence.

Beloved Son. This title signifies Christ's favored, preferential, chosen, and beloved status and also his divine Sonship.

Counselor. The name bears record of his preeminent position among men where the exercise of deliberate judgment and prudence is concerned.

Creator. The creative work of this world and other worlds without number is done by Christ, as he is directed by and uses the power of the Father.

Eternal God. This name signifies that God is from everlasting to everlasting, beyond finite comprehension in power, dominion, godly attributes, and eternal glory.

God of Abraham, Isaac, and Jacob. He appeared to and covenanted with Abraham.

God of Israel. This title signifies his personal, attentive care toward the Israelites.

God of Nature. Through Christ's almighty power, all things in nature are created, upheld, governed, and controlled.

Good Shepherd. His Saints are the sheep, his sheepfold is his Church, and he is the Shepherd.

Holy Messiah. This name signifies his holy and perfected state and his position as Deliverer and King.

Holy One of Israel. He is both the embodiment of holiness and the God of Israel, who came into the world through the lineage of that chosen people.

Husband. Christ (the Bridegroom) shall claim his bride (the Church), celebrate the marriage supper, and become the Husband of his wife.

Immanuel. Christ as God would be born into mortality of a virgin and would be with men to save and redeem them.

Jehovah. This title means God of Israel.

Jesus. Is a masculine personal name meaning Jehovah is salvation or deliverance.

Keeper of the Gate. He shall admit men into the presence of the Father. He opens the gate to the righteous and bars it to the wicked.

King. Christ is the Ruler, Lawgiver, and Sovereign in whom all power rests. As King he rules over the heavens and the earth and all things that are in them.

Lamb of God. He takes away the sin of the world. As a Lamb, he was sacrificed for men, and salvation comes because of the shedding of his blood.

Lord. He is supreme in authority and sovereign over all.

Master. He stood as a teacher, ruler, and commander.

Mediator. One who interposes himself between parties at variance to reconcile them. Christ filled this office as part of his great atoning sacrifice.

Most High. This title designates a state of supreme exaltation in rank, power, and dignity.

Only Begotten Son. Christ is the only Son of the Father in the flesh.

Prince of Peace. In the gospel of Christ are the principles that bring us peace when we obey them.

Prophet. By every test Christ was the greatest of the prophets. He was a teacher, revealer, and witness of the truth.

Redeemer. He ransomed and redeemed men from the effects of the fall of Adam.

Rock. This name carries a connotation of strength and stability.

True Vine. Christ is the True Vine, his Father is the Husbandman, his prophets are the branches, and the fruit which the branches bear is eternal life for the souls of men.

Being aware of the variety of references to the Savior and having an understanding of the rich meanings of each name can inspire reverential awe for our Beloved Redeemer. Nevertheless, the personal witness that the members of the house of Israel desire can be achieved only through a sacred, revealed witness. We can receive the conviction that Jesus is the Christ only when God, the Eternal Father, manifests the truth of it "by the power of the Holy Ghost." (Moroni 10:4.)

To the prayerful, the sincere, and the questioning Jew and Gentile, the Book of Mormon bears a powerful testimony that "Jesus is the Christ, the Eternal God." (Title page.) "The book itself is a new witness for Christ. From first to last it bears record that he is the Son of God and teaches in plainness and perfection the truths of his everlasting gospel. Anyone who believes the Book of Mormon believes in Christ. And conversely, anyone who believes in Christ believes in the Book of Mormon." (Bruce R. McConkie, *The Promised Messiah*, p. 297.)

The amazing variety of names, each used appropriately in its context, provides a powerful witness that the Book of

Mormon is an inspired text. How else can we explain a manuscript of over five hundred pages in which the central figure had 101 positive, divine titles, each title appearing consistently and correctly in its context? Add to this the fact that the central character's name appears nearly four thousand times, on an average of once every 1.7 verses, and the manuscript was translated in less than three months.

Not only does Christ's name appear frequently but there is also much information given in the Book of Mormon about his earthly existence, information that was written in the Americas before his birth in the land of Jerusalem. The prophetic writers of the Book of Mormon seem to have delighted in writing about his earthly existence. They wrote of his coming to earth (1 Nephi 12:6), of his Eternal Father (1 Nephi 11:21), and of his mortal mother (Mosiah 3:8). They wrote of his baptism (2 Nephi 31:4), of his ministry (2 Nephi 2:4), of his disciples (1 Nephi 1:10), of his atonement (Jacob 4:11), of his suffering and death (1 Nephi 10:11), and of his resurrection (2 Nephi 2:8). All this was known to them centuries before the Son of God came to the earth. How did the prophetic writers gain this knowledge? It was theirs because of the righteous lives they had led and the scriptures they had studied and the gift of the Holy Ghost they had sought. The tables below indicate how frequently the prophets wrote in the Book of Mormon of the events that were to occur in Christ's earthly life.

Theme	Number of Appearances
Manifestation *(2 Nephi 25:14)*	39
Son of Eternal Father *(1 Nephi 11:21)*	2
Mary, his mother *(2 Nephi 17:14)*	10
Birth *(1 Nephi 10:4)*	12
John the Baptist *(2 Nephi 31:4)*	6
Baptism *(1 Nephi 10:9)*	9
Chosen Twelve *(1 Nephi 11:35)*	6
Ministry *(1 Nephi 11:24)*	15
Atonement *(1 Nephi 12:10)*	101
Suffering and death *(1 Nephi 11:32–33)*	44
Resurrection *(1 Nephi 10:11)*	34

Theme	1 Nephi	2 Nephi	Jacob	Enos	Jarom	Omni	Mosiah	Alma	Helaman	3 Nephi 1–9
Manifestation	9	6	0	1	0	0	5	7	5	6
Son of Eternal Father	2	0	0	0	0	0	0	0	0	0
Mary, his mother	5	2	0	0	0	0	1	2	0	0
Birth	2	2	1	0	0	0	1	0	6	0
John the Baptist	5	1	0	0	0	0	0	0	0	0
Baptism	3	6	0	0	0	0	0	0	0	0
Chosen Twelve	6	0	0	0	0	0	0	0	0	0
Ministry	5	1	0	0	0	0	6	3	0	0
Atonement	5	26	5	0	0	1	29	26	8	1
Suffering and death	7	9	2	0	0	0	7	8	10	1
Resurrection	1	8	3	0	0	0	10	8	3	1

The central theme the prophetic writers conveyed about Christ was the Atonement. The atoning sacrifice is the key to our returning to our Father in Heaven. The Prophet Joseph Smith said, "All other things which pertain to our religion are only appendages to it." (Teachings of the Prophet Joseph Smith, p. 121.)

By reading the Book of Mormon for information about Christ's earthly existence, we can know that salvation comes to mankind because of the Atonement. Without the atoning sacrifice, the entire plan of salvation would have been thwarted, and the purposes of the Creation, including the populating of this sphere, would come to naught. Because of the atonement of Jesus, we are ransomed from the effects of the fall of Adam, and spiritual and temporal death are overcome through Christ, our victorious Deliverer. The Atonement is his ultimate gift and example.

CONCLUSION

The divinity of Jesus of Nazareth is powerfully proclaimed by prophets in the Book of Mormon. This record, kept by an ancient people living from 600 B.C. to A.D. 421, has come forth as a powerful second witness of Christ. From the time that Lehi left the land of Jerusalem in 600 B.C. until Moroni deposited the plates in the Hill Cumorah in A.D. 421, this account remained in the possession of Lehi and his posterity. The prophets from this lineage wrote of their knowledge, faith, and testimony of the Beloved Son of God. Through the faithful efforts of the prophets and through divine intervention, the promised stick of Joseph, known in latter days as the Book of Mormon, has come forth, as prophesied in Ezekiel: "Behold, I will take the stick of Joseph [the Book of Mormon], which is in the hand of Ephraim, and the tribes of Israel his fellows, and will put them with him, even with the stick of Judah [the Bible], and make them one stick, and they shall be one in mine hand." (Ezekiel 37:19.)

Thus the Book of Mormon came forth to combine with the testimony of the Bible as a witness of the divine mission of Jesus Christ. The words of Christ speak to the soul in irrefutable power. As we begin to know more of Christ, we come to know in a new and more powerful way the promise of Ezekiel.

The stick of Joseph has been available to the Jew and Gentile since 1830. It was translated by a seer chosen "to bring forth my word . . . and not to the bringing forth my word only, saith the Lord, but to the convincing them of my word, which shall have already gone forth among them." (2 Nephi 3:11.) This seer was Joseph Smith, Jr. As a boy he saw a pillar of light directly over his head, above the brightness of the sun, which descended gradually until it fell upon him. When the light rested upon him, he saw two Personages and heard the words, *"This is My Beloved Son. Hear Him!"* (Joseph Smith–History 1:17.) Joseph Smith was prepared — not by man, but by the Lord — to be the translator of this second witness for Jesus Christ. He is known to Latter-day Saints as "a seer, a translator, a prophet, an apostle of Jesus Christ, an elder of the church through the will of God the Father, and the grace of [the] Lord Jesus Christ." (D&C 21:1.)

Through the instrumentality of Joseph Smith, Nephi's intent in writing — "that I may persuade men to come unto the God of Abraham, and the God of Isaac, and the God of Jacob, and be saved" (1 Nephi 6:4) — is now a reality. The intense experience of the "difficulty of engraving . . . words upon plates" (Jacob 4:1) has proven fruitful, and the purpose of the Lord has been fulfilled as the word of God has "come forth unto the Gentiles, by the gift and power of the Lamb" (1 Nephi 13:35).

What the translated word of God means to us is an individual matter. To the critic it will remain a figment of Joseph's imagination. To the friendly scholar it will be a reference point. To the curious it is one more interesting legend. To the well-meaning it is only a history filled with examples of good and bad. But to the seeker after truth and righteousness, the Book of Mormon is a revelation of who God is and stands as a witness that "Jesus is the Christ, the Eternal God." (Title page.)

Chapter 3

BE EVEN AS I AM

*What manner of men ought ye to be? Verily
I say unto you, even as I am.*
3 Nephi 27:27

All scriptures proclaim Jesus Christ as the divine example. The Book of Mormon proclaims in unequaled clarity his life, his attributes, and his doctrine. From searching the Book of Mormon, we can learn in plainness and depth the Christ whom the ancient prophets knew and after whom they patterned their lives.

Many holy men living in the western hemisphere have known of, spoken of, and written of Christ. But only a few have recorded that they personally saw the Holy One of Israel. The brother of Jared saw in vision the Lord and heard, "Behold, I am Jesus Christ." (Ether 3:14.) Father Lehi in a revelatory dream "saw One descending out of the midst of heaven." (1 Nephi 1:9.) Jacob was privileged in his youth to behold the glory of God. (2 Nephi 2:4.) As did Isaiah (2 Nephi 11:2), so did the brother of Jared (Ether 3:14), Lehi (1 Nephi 1:9), Jacob (2 Nephi 2:4), and Nephi (2 Nephi 11:3) know of the Savior, testify of his divine Sonship, write of his forthcoming earthly commission, and have the distinct privilege of seeing the Beloved Son of God (2 Nephi 11:3). Each in his own generation became a witness for Jesus Christ and received a visual manifestation of him.

Christ is accessible not only to the prophets but to earnest inquirers as well. These early prophets realized that the privilege of seeing and directly learning from the Savior would extend beyond themselves to a multitude of men, women, and children in the western hemisphere and even to us in the latter days. A common bond links us with the prophets who proclaim, "And we talk of Christ, we rejoice in Christ, we preach of Christ, we prophesy of Christ, and we write according to our prophecies." (2 Nephi 25:26.)

Surely they looked forward to the day when oneness with Christ would eventually unite all inhabitants of this hemisphere. They must have realized that the persecution they endured for their testimonies of the Lord—Lehi (1 Nephi 1:20), Nephi (1 Nephi 18:12), Aaron (Alma 20:2), and Abinadi (Mosiah 17:20)—would cease because of the sure knowledge of God had by the people. They must have known that the prophetic cry of repentance (Jacob 2:5) and the sealing of testimony with blood (Mosiah 17:20) would not be necessary for almost two hundred years, because a chosen generation had received the sacred privilege of seeing, hearing, and touching the resurrected Redeemer.

Yes, they knew. They looked forward to a singular year for the family of Lehi—a year in which the resurrected Lord would appear to teach and bless their elect posterity.

That year was A.D. 34. Thirty-seven pages of the Book of Mormon were written about A.D. 34. No other year received such attention in writing from the ancient scribes. Contrast the volume of information about this singular year with this lean account of the following years:

"And it came to pass that the seventy and first year passed away, and also the seventy and second year, yea, and in fine, till the seventy and ninth year had passed away; yea, even an hundred years had passed away." (4 Nephi 1:14.)

Why would this one year generate the most prolific account in the Book of Mormon? In this year God, the Exemplar, visited the house of Joseph. The account of this visit is the very centerpiece of the book. The prophets of the Book of Mormon wanted us to enjoy the privilege of learning of this event, for in that year a remnant of the house of Joseph saw, heard, and touched the resurrected Lord and knew, without doubt, the perfect model to follow in their quest for eternal life.

Previously, the privilege of knowing, seeing, and touching the mortal Jesus was limited to persons in the eastern hemisphere. But they did not know with the same sure knowledge of Deity experienced by the people in Bountiful.

There he appeared as a mortal man; here, as a resurrected God.

Despite the fact that in both hemispheres Christ appeared to multitudes, there is a marked contrast in the effect of his appearance on the different groups. In the land of Jerusalem, the Beloved Son of God was born (Matthew 1:23), baptized (Matthew 3:13), crucified (Matthew 20:19), and resurrected (Mark 16:9). Yet most of the multitudes of people who saw and heard him did not know his true identity. They were "astonished [during his youth] at his understanding and answers" (Luke 2:47), acknowledged him as a healer (Mark 1:40–45), feasted on the food he procured (John 6:5–14), and marveled at his casting out of devils from the besieged (Mark 9:25). Yet to them Jesus was not the Son of God. (Luke 4:24.) Their sight was clouded and their hearing impaired, for they did not open their spiritual eyes to ascertain his true identity.

An exception to this general lack of understanding was Peter: "[Christ] saith unto them, But whom say ye that I am? And Simon Peter answered and said, Thou art the Christ, the Son of the living God." (Matthew 16:15–16.)

Like Peter and unlike the people of Judea, the Book of Mormon multitude in A.D. 34 clearly saw, heard, and acknowledged divine instruction from a Man they knew to be the epitome of righteousness — Jesus Christ, the Son of God. That year, A.D. 34, was the year in which multitudes saw and heard the resurrected Lord and recognized him as the Mediator, Redeemer, and the Chosen One of Israel. These same multitudes witnessed the ushering in of a new dispensation founded on the doctrine of Christ. As a result of events of this year, "the people were all converted unto the Lord, upon all the face of the land." (4 Nephi 1:2.) This conversion resulted in nearly two hundred years of continuous peace and prosperity. (4 Nephi 1:22–23.)

The events of A.D. 34 in the western hemisphere will be surpassed only by the events of the year of the second coming of the Savior in clouds of glory. We can view A.D. 34 as the prelude to the symphony that will play at the return of Jesus Christ. Once again multitudes will see, hear, and recognize him as their Deliverer and Messiah. They will witness a new era, a millennial reign based on the doctrines of Christ. Ultimately, every knee shall bow and every tongue confess that Jesus is the Christ. As a result of this acknowledgment, nearly one thousand years will pass in peace, joy, and love.

THE PRELUDE BEGINS: THE MEETING AROUND THE TEMPLE

In the year A.D. 34 a meeting was held around the temple in the land of Bountiful. Approximately twenty-five hundred people gathered. The congregation "consist[ed] of men, women, and children." (3 Nephi 17:25.) It appears that they gathered as families with their "sick and their afflicted, and their lame, and with their blind, and with their dumb, and with all them that were afflicted in any manner." (3 Nephi 17:9.) At this family gathering, the only person identified was the prophet Nephi, who was the first man called forth by Christ: "And it came to pass that he spake unto Nephi (for Nephi was among the multitude) and he commanded him that he should come forth. And Nephi arose and went forth, and bowed himself before the Lord and did kiss his feet." (3 Nephi 11:18–19.)

Why was Nephi known? It was because of his righteousness. Before A.D. 34 he had "been visited by angels and also the voice of the Lord, therefore having seen angels, and being eye-witness, and having had power given unto him that he might know concerning the ministry of Christ." (3 Nephi 7:15.) Further, he had gone forth and testified, "boldly, repentance and remission of sins through faith on the Lord Jesus Christ." (3 Nephi 7:16.) Nephi had ministered "with power and with great authority" (3 Nephi 7:17), even to the casting out of "devils and unclean spirits; and even his brother did he raise from the dead, after he had been stoned and suffered death by the people" (3 Nephi 7:19). Nephi becomes to us another example of righteousness.

When the great prophet Nephi and his people gathered in Bountiful, the people conversed with each other on two topics that dominated their conversations. The first concerned the changes that had taken place on the earth (3 Nephi 11:1): the great city of Zarahemla had been burned with fire (3 Nephi 8:8), the city of Moroni had sunk in the

depths of the sea (3 Nephi 8:9), the city of Moronihah had
been covered with earth (3 Nephi 8:10), and highways had
been broken up (3 Nephi 8:13). It was, in essence, a conversation about "the face of the whole earth [becoming]
deformed." (3 Nephi 8:17.) The second topic of conversation was of more eternal importance. It concerned the
"sign [which] had been given concerning his [Christ's]
death." (3 Nephi 11:2.)

Notably, no one person appears to have conducted the
flow of the conversation. There was not a speaker or a
tower to look at, as with King Benjamin. (Mosiah 2.) No
one appeared to be presiding, conducting, or speaking,
even though the prophet Nephi was among their number.
(3 Nephi 11:18.) It was as if they were conversing, waiting,
as it were, for the meeting to commence, or waiting to know
for what purpose they had come to the temple at this particular time with their families.

Any questions of who was to preside were put to rest
when God the Father addressed the gathering. (3 Nephi
11:3.) He did not wait for silence or for their attention as
they conversed. They heard a piercing voice, which was
audible, yet which they did not understand. A second time
they heard the voice, but again they did not understand it.
(3 Nephi 11:4.) Was it because the Lord did not speak
plainly? No, it was because the people needed the veil over
their minds and hearts removed.

A third time the divine parental voice spoke, and this
time the assembly understood: "Behold my Beloved Son, in
whom I am well pleased, in whom I have glorified my
name—hear ye him." (3 Nephi 11:7.) They gazed toward
heaven to hear the words of God the Father and in their
gazing became witnesses of the glorious descent of Jesus
Christ to the land of Joseph. (3 Nephi 11:8.)

Although the veil had been lifted from the people's
minds, ears, and eyes, for they could understand the voice
and see the personage, it is apparent their understanding
was yet clouded. The multitude wrongfully concluded that
the man clothed in white and descending toward them was
an angel, not Jesus Christ, of whom the prophets had testified. (3 Nephi 11:8.)

Why did this mistaken identity occur? Perhaps the multitude had known of him but did not know him. An exception was the prophet Nephi, who had previously received the gift to know. (3 Nephi 7:15.) Was it Nephi, then, who increased their enlightenment? No, it was their Savior, their Redeemer, their God, Jesus the Christ. He announced, "Behold, I am Jesus Christ, whom the prophets testified shall come into the world." (3 Nephi 11:10.)

The effect of this announcement was not a shout for joy but what I would term a "sacred silence." As if the people might need a further divine affirmation to understand the full import of the name he had stated, the risen Lord told them something of his earthly ministry in Jerusalem. He did not give information about his birth, his baptism, his choosing of the Twelve, his crucifixion, or his resurrection. What he described was the Atonement. "[I] have glorified the Father in taking upon me the sins of the world, in the which I have suffered the will of the Father in all things from the beginning." (3 Nephi 11:11.)

Why did the resurrected Lord speak of the Atonement to further assure the multitude of his identity? It was because the Atonement was the central message of Christ's earthly ministry. It was because he wanted them to know of his great gift to all. The Atonement is the very thread that binds the plan of happiness. It is the most important doctrine of the gospel. Prophets, scribes, and writers in the Book of Mormon wrote of this doctrine more frequently than they wrote of any other single concept relating to the life of the Nazarene.

From this point the multitude knew who was presiding and who was conducting, and they were now to learn why they had gathered around the temple at Bountiful. The purpose was not only to see the man Jesus as those in Jerusalem had seen him but also to receive a sure knowledge that the Man conducting this meeting was the very Christ, the Son of God, the Savior of the world.

The risen Lord in charitable magnitude invited the multitude to come and become sure witnesses of him. They were invited to thrust their hands into his side and feel the prints of the nails in his hands and feet. (3 Nephi 11:14.) Notice the verbs used—*thrust* and *felt*. To the senses of sight and hearing already involved in this witnessing process was to be added the sense of touch. An experience involving only one sense, such as sight, could be counterfeited or in some other way remain open to question. But the three together were decisive, and they led to a spiritual knowledge that went beyond the physical.

The significance is heightened as we realize the time Jesus spent with the multitude in offering this sacred privilege. If only 2,500 people went "forth one by one until they had all gone forth, and did see with their eyes and did feel with their hands, and did know of a surety and did bear record" (3 Nephi 11:15), each taking five seconds, 12 people would complete the process in one minute. In one hour, at this rate, 720 people would be sure witnesses; in three hours 2,260 people would have completed the process. What if each person took longer than five seconds? What if each one took ten seconds or a minute? Marvelous is the magnitude of the event at which the Savior presided, so that a diverse multitude of families could share together the sacred privilege of touching their Redeemer.

Whatever the time involved, we know that when it was completed, the multitude shouted in one accord, or in complete unity, "Hosanna! Blessed be the name of the Most High God!" Then the multitude "did fall down at the feet of Jesus, and did worship him." (3 Nephi 11:17.) A multitude now possessed a sure witness to what the prophets had testified since the beginning of time.

THE PRELUDE CONTINUES:
A NEW DISPENSATION

After establishing a multitude of witnesses, the Savior began a new dispensation in the land of Joseph. Establishing this dispensation seems to have been the main purpose of the Lord's ministry in the western hemisphere.

The First Day

Christ established his authority. Christ chose from among the multitude twelve righteous men to be his disciples. He selected them in the view of the entire multitude in contrast to the selection of the twelve in Jerusalem, which may not have been done in view of a multitude. This difference illustrates the righteous state of the people in the western hemisphere, as compared with that of the multitudes in Jerusalem.

After he gave the twelve disciples authority, the Lord emphasized the significant role of the twelve by giving them specific instructions apart from the instructions he gave to the multitude. Nine specific instructions for the twelve are recorded, and twenty-seven instructions for the multitude. One way of viewing this difference is that the multitude received three times as many specific assignments. Another way to view the difference is that the twelve received thirty-six assignments compared to the twenty-seven given to the multitude.

Whatever way we view the assignments, the important concept is the content of the message to each. Christ removed all doubt that a divine calling had been given to the twelve when he declared: "Blessed are ye if ye shall give heed unto the words of these twelve." (3 Nephi 12:1.)

Doctrine for this dispensation was taught. Christ's teachings in the land of Bountiful on the first day of his visit are compiled in three short chapters, 3 Nephi 12 through 14. At the end of the day, the Savior said, "Behold, ye have heard the things which I taught before I ascended to my Father." (3 Nephi 15:1; see also Matthew, Mark, Luke, and John.) In other words, the multitude had listened to the teachings from the Lord's earthly ministry in Jerusalem. The simplicity of these brief chapters is evidenced in the abridgment of Mormon. "And now there cannot be written in this book even a hundredth part of the things which Jesus did truly teach unto the people." (3 Nephi 26:6.) Yet the path as abridged in the Book of Mormon in three chapters is more clearly paved than in the New Testament. Noticeably missing from the Lord's ministry in Bountiful were the hecklers, the hypocrites, the Sadducees who taunted Christ throughout his ministry in Jerusalem. Their absence allowed him to speak plainly to the assembled multitude.

After his gospel discourse the Savior looked upon the multitude and perceived that the people were still weak in gospel understanding, even though they had seen the risen Messiah and had heard his teachings. He perceived that they could not understand all the words his Father had commanded him to speak, even though they had been spoken in plainness. The exception to this observation was the twelve. They understood, and they would begin to teach the people on the following day with the "same words which Jesus had spoken—nothing varying from the words which Jesus had spoken." (3 Nephi 19:8.)

The power of the priesthood was shown forth. The Lord told the people to go to their homes and prepare their minds for the second day of his ministry by pondering his teachings and praying to their Father in Heaven. Despite his commandment to return to their homes, however, the people lingered. With tear-filled eyes, they steadfastly gazed upon him. (3 Nephi 17:1-5.) He perceived that the multitude desired to be recipients of the power of the priesthood. The Lord demonstrated his power humbly, for he stated, "I see that your faith is sufficient that I should heal you." (3 Nephi 17:8.) He healed the lame, the blind, the withered, and all those who were afflicted. (3 Nephi 17:9.) The formerly afflicted, now whole, bathed the resurrected Redeemer's feet with their tears. (3 Nephi 17:10.)

This vivid, touching scene grew more tender when the Holy One blessed the little children among the assembly. Though Christ had blessed children in Jerusalem, the New Testament account of this act seems painfully sparse when compared to the moving portrayal in the Book of Mormon. The Master invited the people to bring their children to him. (3 Nephi 17:11.) Then, kneeling with the multitude, he humbly prayed to his Father. (3 Nephi 17:15.) After his prayer, the Savior blessed each child one by one, weeping as he did so. (3 Nephi 17:21.) A celestial fire surrounded the little ones, the heavens opened, and the angels descended to minister unto the blessed children. (3 Nephi 17:24.)

The sacrament was administered. The Savior continued his loving ministry by instituting the sacrament. In Jerusalem he had fed the multitude with loaves and fishes; but only to his apostles assembled in the upper room on the Feast of the Passover had he administered the sacred sacrament of bread and wine. (Matthew 26:26–29.) In Bountiful, the Savior extended this blessing to all. The bread he broke and blessed and gave to the twelve; these, having eaten, distributed the emblems to the multitude. (3 Nephi 26:13.)

The Lord made very plain the sanctity and significance of the ordinance of the sacrament. The sacred writings of the Book of Mormon give us the most perfect recitation we have of the meaning and purpose of the sacrament.

The power to give the gift of the Holy Ghost was conferred upon the twelve disciples. As a final display of his Sonship on that first day, Christ gave his disciples the power to give the gift of the Holy Ghost. The prophet Nephi stated that the Holy Ghost "is the gift of God unto all those who diligently seek him, as well in times of old as in the time that he should manifest himself unto the children of men." (1 Nephi 10:17.)

The Second Day

The covenant of baptism was instituted. The second day began with the people's listening to the words of the chosen twelve. (3 Nephi 19:6.) For many, the words were a repetition of the words they had heard the Savior speak the previous day. The multitude not only listened to sacred words but also watched as Nephi instituted the sacred covenant of baptism by baptizing the twelve disciples. (3 Nephi 19:12.) After they were baptized, "they were encircled about . . . by fire; and it came down from heaven, and the multitude did witness it, and did bear record; and angels did come down out of heaven and did minister unto them. . . . Jesus came and stood in the midst and ministered unto them." (3 Nephi 19:14–15.)

Christ prayed unto the Father. After the Savior had ministered to his disciples, he turned in view of the multitude and began to commune with his Father. Kneeling in prayer, Christ with gratitude thanked his Father for giving to his disciples the Holy Ghost. (3 Nephi 19:20.) With heartfelt desire he then asked that his Father give the Holy Ghost to all who would believe the words of his disciples. (3 Nephi 19:21.) While Jesus communed with his Father, the multitude and the disciples began to pray. The Lord, observing their faithfulness, shined his countenance upon them, and the disciples became as white as Christ's own countenance and apparel. (3 Nephi 19:25.) The Redeemer then knelt and gratefully prayed. (3 Nephi 19:28.)

The multitude heard the prayer, recorded it in their

hearts, and understood the words expressed. (3 Nephi 19:33.) The information contained in the third prayer given on the second day is not recorded in the Book of Mormon; however, Christ commented after the final prayer that is recorded: "So great faith have I never seen among all the Jews; wherefore I could not show unto them so great miracles, because of their unbelief." (3 Nephi 19:35.)

The ordinance of the sacrament was repeated. After the third prayer, the Savior broke sacramental bread and gave wine to the multitude. (3 Nephi 20:3–6.) The sacred emblems were not procured by man but by divine action. After partaking of the holy sacrament, the multitude cried with one voice, giving glory to Jesus Christ, the procurer of the emblems. (3 Nephi 20:9.)

The resurrected Lord read from holy scripture. The Lord chose first to expound the words of Isaiah. (3 Nephi 20:11.) Christ commanded the people to search the words of Isaiah, for Isaiah's writings masterfully describe the remnant of Jacob and explain how this remnant will come to a knowledge of the Lord their God and inherit the lands of Joseph. (1 Nephi 20:11–13.) Christ emphasized that Israel would be gathered at the coming forth of the Book of Mormon and that the Gentiles would be established as a free people in the promised land. He indicated that the Gentiles would be saved if they would believe and obey the words of Christ; otherwise they would be cut off and destroyed. And he expounded the writings of Isaiah that spoke of the building of the new Jerusalem, the return of the lost ten tribes, and the merciful gathering of Israel. (3 Nephi 21.)

The Lord wanted the people to search the teachings of other prophets as well as the words of Isaiah. He explained, "Search the prophets, for many there be that testify of these things." (3 Nephi 23:5.) The other prophets whom Christ specifically mentioned included Samuel the Lamanite (3 Nephi 23:9) and Malachi (3 Nephi 24:1). The Lord wanted Samuel's prophecy regarding the Saints' rising from the dead, appearing to many, and ministering to the people of Joseph to be included in Nephite scripture. (3 Nephi 23:9.) From the words of Malachi, the Savior emphasized that a messenger would prepare the way for his second coming to the earth. (3 Nephi 24.)

The Lord's conclusion, therefore, to the second day of his ministry was to enlighten the minds of the people to the truth contained in holy writ: "And he did expound all things, even from the beginning until the time that he should come in his glory—yea, even all things which should come upon the face of the earth, even until the elements should melt with fervent heat, and the earth should be wrapt together as a scroll, and the heavens and the earth should pass away." (3 Nephi 26:3.)

The Third Day

The third day of Christ's ministry raises many questions that remain unanswered. It is not known how Christ came to the land of Bountiful on the third day. On the first day, he descended from heaven; on the second day, he was first seen ministering to the twelve. How did he descend the third day? What did he teach on the third day? On the first day he had expanded and clarified the teachings taught in his three-year ministry among the people in Jerusalem. On the second day he had expounded the scriptures and told what would happen in the latter days. What new words did he have on the third day? (3 Nephi 26:16.) From Mormon we learn "that the Lord truly did teach the people, for the space of three days; and after that he did show himself unto them oft, and did break bread oft, and bless it, and give it unto them." (3 Nephi 26:13.) Perhaps when the house of Israel faithfully adheres to the teachings of the first two days of the risen Lord's American ministry, the unanswered questions of the third day of his ministry will be made manifest.

As witnesses for the new dispensation, the multitude had observed—

1. The establishment of priesthood authority among their number.

2. The teaching of the doctrine for the new dispensation.

3. The marvelous, divine power of the priesthood to bless the lives of all.

4. The ordinance of the sacrament being administered.

5. The chosen disciples receiving power to give the gift of the Holy Ghost.

6. The chosen twelve being baptized and being administered to by the Savior and heavenly angels.

7. Christ pray to God the Father.

8. The repetition of the ordinance of the sacrament.

9. The recitation of prophecies.

This multitude was truly blessed. Where else do the scriptures speak of a more blessed multitude than the one gathered at the temple in Bountiful in A.D. 34? Nowhere can we find a gathering or a meeting of multitudes that surpasses this gathering of the people living on the western hemisphere. Yet what they saw, what they heard, and what they felt as they witnessed the Savior and the ushering in of a new dispensation is only a prelude to the symphony that will play in the year of the second coming of the Messiah.

THE PRELUDE CONCLUDES

Following the resurrected Lord's three-day ministry, many great and marvelous applications of his teachings occurred. By A.D. 36, all the people in the land were converted, for so great were the witness and testimony that the love of God dwelt within every heart. No longer were there whoredoms, lyings, murders, contentions or disputations, or any manner of lasciviousness, but all of the people in the land of Joseph dealt justly with each other. (4 Nephi 1:2.) The Lord blessed them, and they prospered in the land, and they rebuilt their cities. (4 Nephi 1:7.) They multiplied exceedingly, insomuch that the whole face of the land was inhabited, and they were a fair and a delightsome people. (4 Nephi 1:10.) So great was the faith of the people that they practiced the law of consecration and had all things in common. (4 Nephi 1:3.) No longer were there racial, social, economic, or political divisions of any kind in the land. (4 Nephi 1:17.) They were a purified people, united in their knowledge and understanding of Jesus Christ.

The disciples whom the Lord had chosen performed great and marvelous miracles among the people. They healed the sick and the infirm and raised the dead—all in the name of Jesus Christ. (4 Nephi 1:5.) No longer did the people follow the law of Moses; instead, they lived the higher law proclaimed by the Lord Jesus in this new dispensation. For more than 150 years after the ascension of the Master, there was peace and harmony in the land of Joseph, resulting in generations passing away in righteousness. (4 Nephi

1:22.) The people experienced the greatest happiness known on earth. (4 Nephi 1:16.) This happiness was brought about by the people's living in accordance with righteous principles set forth in the new dispensation. This great blessing was brought to the people in A.D. 34 by the Son of God in fulfillment of his divine appointment.

The same teachings and blessings are available to the righteous in the dispensation of the fulness of times that were enjoyed by those gathered at the temple in Bountiful in A.D. 34. The Lord has chosen his latter-day disciples and given them the power to direct his church upon the earth. His chosen latter-day twelve have been baptized, and they now baptize others, because the divine power of the priesthood has been restored once again. The doctrine of Christ has been revealed anew. The right to partake of the sacrament has been returned. By the authority of God the sick and afflicted are healed and little children are blessed. Through the Book of Mormon the fulness of Christ's gospel is proclaimed and the priesthood pattern for the righteous is shown forth.

Chapter 4

CHRIST,
THE GREAT I AM

God said unto Moses, I AM THAT I AM.
Exodus 3:14

We are promised that by implementing the teachings of our Savior we can experience a "mighty change" of heart. (Alma 5:12.) Yet even Saints wonder if the "mighty change" has occurred as they notice the gap between their knowledge, actions, and conversion. So the question arises, what is preventing us from becoming the person that we want to be?

The answer to this soul-searching query is suggested by the song "I Am a Child of God." (*Hymns of The Church of Jesus Christ of Latter-day Saints*, 1985, no. 301.) As the song was originally composed, one phrase was "Teach me all that I must *know* / To live with him someday." (Italics added.) Many Saints made mental note of all of the encyclopedic minutia of the gospel as if merely knowing would result in living "with him someday." Answers to such questions as how wide is the Sea of Galilee, what are the variety of fishes within the Sea of Galilee, or how many steps would Christ have walked with his cross may have seemed all-important to our salvation.

Then the phrase was changed to "Teach me all that I must *do* / To live with him someday." (Italics added.) Saints began the *Do it*s, attempting to have their actions match their knowledge. They recognized that it was not enough to define faith; faithful actions were needed to obtain salvation.

It was not enough to define service; service must be rendered to obtain salvation.

Discovering the centrality of Christ in the Book of Mormon can lead us to imagine yet another change in the lyrics of the song. The new words might be "Teach me all that I must *be* / To live with him someday." (Italics added.) A form of the verb "to be" is "I am."

When Christ appeared to Moses, Moses asked him, "Behold, when I come unto the children of Israel, and shall say unto them, The God of your fathers hath sent me unto you; and they shall say to me, What is his name? what shall I say unto them? And God said unto Moses, I AM THAT I AM." (Exodus 3:13–14.) It is not enough to *know* or even to *do*, but we must truly *be*, even as *I AM*.

Pondering this idea may lead us to recognize that the only persons who ever ask us "*Are you* the principle you espouse?" are our bishop and a member of the stake presidency at our temple recommend interview. It would be convenient if they merely asked, "What do you know about tithing?" Or even, "Do you do tithing acts?" Then we could quickly respond with the appropriate definition and describe one day on which we gave 10 percent of our means to help another. Or what if they asked, "Can you define morality?" Or even, "Do you do moral acts?" Then we could readily share with our priesthood leaders the knowledge we have of morality and chastity and relate an experience in our lives when we did a very moral act. But this convenient form of questioning would not bring about the "mighty change" of heart we seek.

The questions of the temple recommend interview center on "Are you . . . ?" In order to obtain the desired recommend we must soul-searchingly respond as our Savior did and finally say, "I am." In other words, whether it is a Sunday, a Friday night, or a holiday, we must, with all our heart, as well as with all our mind and strength, be constantly as he is.

Unfortunately, as we try to implement the teachings of our Savior recorded by the Book of Mormon prophets, we recognize our weaknesses and our failure to be even as he is. We recognize that our weaknesses are mirrored in those of the majority spoken of in the Book of Mormon—a majority who once loved God but who eventually rejected him. They failed to be as he is. Their repetitive pattern of repentance, acceptance of the gospel, and enjoyment of the blessings it brings was only momentary. Pride, pollution, lasciviousness, and vengeful hatred found permanence in their hearts. Their own willful choice led to their eventual demise, both in earthly joys and in eternal blessings.

Could it be that Moroni and Mormon, the great prophets and abridgers, recorded these recurrent failure patterns for instruction in our day? Moroni wrote: "Behold, I speak unto you as if ye were present. . . . Jesus Christ hath shown you unto me, and I know your doing. . . . And I know that ye do walk in the pride of your hearts. . . . Why are ye ashamed to take upon you the name of Christ?" (Mormon 8:35–38.)

Was he speaking to us? How can we avoid pride (being ashamed of Christ) and love the Lord with all our heart, mind, and strength?

First, we need to know of him, who he is, what kind of being he is, and what his attributes and characteristics are. The Prophet Joseph Smith stated in 1844, "I want to ask this congregation, every man, woman and child, to answer the question in their own heart, what kind of a being God is?" (Teachings of the Prophet Joseph Smith, p. 343.) Without doubt, the Prophet Joseph Smith knew the answer by divine revelation, and he further knew that each individual needed to come to a true knowledge of the nature of God. Second, we need to do the works of our Savior. Third, we need to be even as he is. The Book of Mormon is our guide in the process of achieving the "mighty change" of heart.

THE DIVINE NATURE OF
"I AM THAT I AM"

The Book of Mormon is filled with seemingly endless illustrations of the loving kindness, long-suffering, and infinite goodness extended by the Lord toward his often erring people. It was the Lord God Almighty who guided Lehi, the brother of Jared, and the people of Mulek to the promised land. It was the Lord who called prophets to serve continually in the midst of his prideful people. It was the Lord who constantly directed his holy prophets to share with the vast, mostly carnal majority the sure knowledge of the Beloved Savior and the divine word of God. It was the God of Abraham, Isaac, and Jacob who instructed prophets to organize churches, to administer the saving ordinance of baptism, and to ordain priesthood brethren among the sometimes repentant. It was the Lord of Hosts who used war, famine, pestilence, and poverty to chastise the people and make them humble so that they might repent and incline themselves to the teachings of salvation. It was the Eternal Father who sent his glorified, resurrected Son to minister to the weak but willing remnant of his people.

The Lord was vitally interested in the wayward multitudes on the western hemisphere. He was not an absentee God or a vengeful God to them. Nor is he to us. He is a living God, a God who possesses a body. The Lord, when showing his perfect body to the brother of Jared, declared, "Seest thou that ye are created after mine own image? Yea, even all men were created in the beginning after mine own image." (Ether 3:15.)

Joseph Smith reiterated this truth: "If the veil were rent today, and the great God who holds this world in its orbit, and who upholds all worlds and all things by his power, was to make himself visible, — I say, if you were to see him today, you would see him like a man in form — like yourselves in all the person, image, and very form as a man." (*Teachings of the Prophet Joseph Smith*, p. 345.)

The reason God was seen in the form of a man is that he is a man: "Man of Holiness is his name." (Moses 6:57.)

References to God's having body parts occur 283 times in the Book of Mormon. He used his body to assist and benefit the ancient inhabitants. For example, the Lord symbolically used his hands to guide (2 Nephi 1:24) and to recover (2 Nephi 21:11) his children. He used his voice, his mouth, and his tongue to converse with his chosen people (Helaman 5:30), to chasten them (1 Nephi 16:25), and to command them (1 Nephi 3:2). He used his mighty arms to protect (Enos 1:13) and to receive (Mormon 6:17) his Saints. He used his eyes to search (2 Nephi 9:44) and to pierce (Jacob 2:10) the heart of man.

God possesses a body / Specific verse	1 Nephi	2 Nephi	Jacob	Enos	Jarom	Omni	Words of Mormon	Mosiah	Alma	Helaman	3 Nephi	4 Nephi	Mormon	Ether	Moroni	Line total	Category total
Arm — 1 Nephi 20:14	3	5	2	0	0	1	0	3	2	0	1	0	0	0	0	17	
arms — 2 Nephi 1:15	0	1	0	0	0	0	0	2	2	0	0	0	0	0	0	5	
holy arm — Enos 1:13	0	0	0	1	0	0	0	2	0	0	1	0	0	0	0	4	
open arms — Mormon 6:17	0	0	0	0	0	0	0	0	0	0	0	1	0	0	0	1	27
Back — 2 Nephi 7:6	0	1	0	0	0	0	0	0	0	0	0	0	0	0	0	1	1
Blood — Alma 5:21	0	0	0	0	0	0	0	0	6	0	0	0	1	5	2	14	14
Bowels — Mosiah 15:9	0	0	0	0	0	0	0	1	3	0	2	0	0	0	0	6	6
Cheeks — 2 Nephi 7:6	0	1	0	0	0	0	0	0	0	0	0	0	0	0	0	1	1
Ear — 2 Nephi 7:5	0	2	0	0	0	0	0	0	0	0	0	0	0	0	0	2	
ears — 2 Nephi 15:9	0	2	0	0	0	0	0	0	0	0	0	0	0	0	0	2	4

God possesses a body	Specific verse	1 Nephi	2 Nephi	Jacob	Enos	Jarom	Omni	Words of Mormon	Mosiah	Alma	Helaman	3 Nephi	4 Nephi	Mormon	Ether	Moroni	Line total	Category total
Eye	Jacob 2:15	0	0	1	0	0	0	0	0	0	0	0	0	0	0	0	1	
all-searching eye	2 Nephi 9:44	0	1	0	0	0	0	0	0	0	0	0	0	0	0	0	1	
eyes	2 Nephi 3:8	0	3	0	0	0	0	0	0	0	0	0	0	0	0	0	3	
eyes of his glory	2 Nephi 13:8	0	1	0	0	0	0	0	0	0	0	0	0	0	0	0	1	
piercing eye	Jacob 2:10	0	0	1	0	0	0	0	0	0	0	0	0	0	0	0	1	7
Face	2 Nephi 7:6	0	3	0	0	0	0	0	0	0	0	5	0	0	0	0	8	8
Feet	3 Nephi 11:15	0	0	0	0	0	0	0	0	0	0	7	0	0	0	0	7	7
Finger	Alma 10:2	0	0	0	0	0	0	0	0	1	0	0	0	0	10	0	11	11
Flesh	Alma 7:12	0	0	0	0	0	0	0	0	3	0	0	0	0	5	1	9	9
Hand	1 Nephi 20:13	3	19	4	0	0	1	0	6	10	0	2	1	2	4	1	53	

Term	Reference														Total	
hands	2 Nephi 1:24	0	3	1	0	0	2	9	0	2	0	1	0	0	18	84
left hand	Mosiah 5:10	0	0	0	0	0	2	0	0	0	0	0	0	0	2	2
palms of my hands	1 Nephi 21:16	1	0	0	0	0	0	0	0	0	0	0	0	0	1	2
right hand	1 Nephi 20:13	1	1	0	0	0	2	2	1	0	0	0	1	2	10	14
Lips	2 Nephi 21:4	0	2	0	0	0	0	0	0	0	0	0	0	0	2	1
Loins	2 Nephi 21:5	0	2	0	0	0	0	0	0	0	0	0	0	0	2	1
Mouth	2 Nephi 3:21	0	7	0	0	0	3	0	0	1	0	0	0	3	14	1
Shoulder	2 Nephi 19:6	0	1	0	0	0	0	0	0	0	0	0	0	0	1	
Side	3 Nephi 11:14	0	0	0	0	0	0	0	0	1	0	0	0	0	1	
Tongue	2 Nephi 7:4	0	1	0	0	0	0	0	0	0	0	0	0	0	1	
Voice	1 Nephi 16:25	10	5	2	2	0	7	11	14	18	0	1	1	0	73	
mighty voice	Alma 5:51	0	0	0	0	0	0	1	0	0	0	0	0	0	1	
mildness of the voice	Helaman 5:31	0	0	0	0	0	0	0	1	0	0	0	0	0	1	

God possesses a body — *Specific verse*	1 Nephi	2 Nephi	Jacob	Enos	Jarom	Omni	Words of Mormon	Mosiah	Alma	Helaman	3 Nephi	4 Nephi	Mormon	Ether	Moroni	Line total	Category total
pleasant voice *Helaman 5:46*	0	0	0	0	0	0	0	0	0	1	0	0	0	0	0	1	
small voice *3 Nephi 11:3*	0	0	0	0	0	0	0	0	0	0	1	0	0	0	0	1	
still small voice *1 Nephi 17:45*	1	0	0	0	0	0	0	0	0	0	0	0	0	0	0	1	
still voice of perfect mildness *Helaman 5:30*	0	0	0	0	0	0	0	0	0	1	0	0	0	0	0	1	
voice of a great tumultuous noise *Helaman 5:30*	0	0	0	0	0	0	0	0	0	1	0	0	0	0	0	1	
voice of thunder *1 Nephi 17:45*	1	0	0	0	0	0	0	0	0	1	1	0	0	0	0	3	
TOTALS	20	61	11	3	0	4	0	30	50	20	42	2	5	26	9	283	83

He is not only a living God who possesses a body but also a God who has divine passions. References to God's having passions are made in 320 verses in the Book of Mormon. The deep emotions involving the Lord's attributes of merciful love were recorded 221 times, whereas the loving, yet judgmental, passions of God were recorded 99 times. This illustrates that the Lord showed forth doubly his passions of a merciful, loving nature as compared to his passions of a judgmental nature. This ratio is of particular significance, for the Lord showed forth far more nurturing than correcting passions, even though the multitudes chose to reject him.

The Lord's passions are not diluted by reasoning or compromise but are powerful, intense, and sure. They are not all of one hue but are a full palate of emotion that stirs the heart. His passions are always appropriate, controlled, and directed to assist toward life eternal all who choose to obey.

These passions, so clearly revealed in the Book of Mormon, appear to have been predicated on the actions of the people. When the people kept the commandments, gave willing service to others, and set their course toward eternal life, the emotions that God revealed to them were love (1 Nephi 11:22), goodness (1 Nephi 1:1), comfort (2 Nephi 8:3), patience (Mosiah 4:6), and mercy (1 Nephi 1:14). The strictness with which the people turned their hearts, minds, strength, and devotions to the Lord obviously determined the extent and degree of the loving passions he showed to them. (4 Nephi.)

During times when the people were not valiant and yet had not severely hardened their hearts, the Lord showed forth abundant offers of mercy, the blessing of time to repent, and the loving leadership of mighty prophets. The Lord extended his arms of mercy even into the night of darkened hearts and wandering minds.

Yet when the people of the Book of Mormon flagrantly chose to rebel against the counsel of God, to live in wickedness, and to thwart the gospel plan, the passions of displeasure (2 Nephi 1:22), anger (1 Nephi 20:9), and wrath (1 Nephi 13:11) were prominent in God's dealings with them. The degree to which the people were disobedient to

God determined their judgment. (Alma 36:15.) Thus, when the vast majority rejected God and willfully rebelled against his words, they felt God's fiery indignation, fierce anger, and almighty wrath — the eternal emotions that would result in the multitudes' damnation.

Obedience is clearly what we should choose. What hope this message brings. Our God, our Redeemer, has a body of parts and passions. He uses his body to assist us as we traverse today's battlefields, lightening the course to strength and victory. His passions give assurance in an age that denies emotions on one extreme and exploits them on the other, or turns up emotional volume without direction with drugs, or turns down volume with despair. Christ does not deny his passions but magnifies them in complete willingness to serve, to lead, to bless all his children, not with a quiet whisper but with a certain, clarion call. All we need to do is obey.

The pattern is clear. Christ extends his tender mercies. He pleads. He teaches. He assists. He challenges. He chastises. He corrects. He blesses. He waits and hopes for our repentance. We cannot claim or purport that the Lord is not interested in us, nor that God is an absentee Father, nor that he has made no effort to redeem us. Thus as followers of Christ, we need to be as he is. The distracted youth, the uninterested adult, the wandering elder, the discouraged grandparent, the angry apostate need our love. It is not enough to know or even to do. We must be as he is.

God possesses passions: Loving attributes — Specific verse	1 Nephi	2 Nephi	Jacob	Enos	Jarom	Omni	Words of Mormon	Mosiah	Alma	Helaman	3 Nephi	4 Nephi	Mormon	Ether	Moroni	Line total	Category total
Comfort — 2 Nephi 8:3	0	3	0	0	0	0	0	0	4	0	0	0	0	0	0	7	
comforted — 1 Nephi 21:13	1	1	0	0	0	0	0	2	3	0	1	0	0	0	0	8	
comfortedst — 2 Nephi 22:1	0	1	0	0	0	0	0	0	0	0	0	0	0	0	0	1	
comforteth — 2 Nephi 8:12	0	1	0	0	0	0	0	0	0	0	0	0	0	0	0	1	
compassion — Mosiah 15:9	0	0	0	0	0	0	0	1	0	0	2	0	0	3	0	6	
pity — Ether 3:3	0	0	0	0	0	0	0	0	0	0	0	0	0	1	0	1	24
Goodness — 1 Nephi 1:1	3	4	1	0	0	0	0	5	4	0	0	0	2	0	0	19	
exceeding goodness — Alma 60:11	0	0	0	0	0	0	0	0	1	0	0	0	0	0	0	1	
good — Moroni 7:12	0	0	0	0	0	0	0	0	0	0	0	0	0	0	5	5	
great goodness — 2 Nephi 4:17	0	1	0	0	0	0	0	0	0	1	1	0	0	0	0	3	

God possesses passions:
Loving attributes
Specific verse

Attribute (verse)	Category total	Line total	Moroni	Ether	Mormon	4 Nephi	3 Nephi	Helaman	Alma	Mosiah	Words of Mormon	Omni	Jarom	Enos	Jacob	2 Nephi	1 Nephi
great infinite goodness *Helaman 12:1*		1	0	0	0	0	0	1	0	0	0	0	0	0	0	0	0
immediate goodness *Mosiah 25:10*		1	0	0	0	0	0	0	0	1	0	0	0	0	0	0	0
infinite goodness *2 Nephi 1:10*	33	3	1	0	0	0	0	0	0	1	0	0	0	0	0	1	0
Joy *2 Nephi 19:17*		5	0	0	0	0	1	0	0	0	0	0	0	0	3	1	0
pleased *Mosiah 14:10*		1	0	0	0	0	0	0	0	1	0	0	0	0	0	0	0
pleasure *Jacob 4:9*		4	0	0	0	0	0	0	0	2	0	0	0	0	2	0	0
rejoice exceedingly *Jacob 5:60*		1	0	0	0	0	0	0	0	0	0	0	0	1	0	0	0
Love *1 Nephi 11:22*	11	13	0	1	1	1	0	0	1	1	0	0	0	0	2	2	4
loved *Helaman 15:3*		3	0	1	0	0	0	1	0	0	0	0	0	0	0	0	1
loveth *1 Nephi 11:17*		6	0	0	0	0	0	1	2	0	0	0	0	0	0	1	2

Phrase		1	2	3	4	5	6	7	8	9	10	11	12	Total
														24
loving kindness	*1 Nephi 19:9*	1	0	0	0	0	0	0	0	0	0	0	0	1
matchless bounty of his love	*Alma 26:15*	0	0	0	0	0	0	1	0	0	0	0	0	1
Mercy	*1 Nephi 1:14*	3	8	1	0	0	10	27	1	2	1	1	3	57
abundant mercy	*Alma 18:41*	0	0	0	0	0	0	1	0	0	0	0	0	1
exceedingly merciful	*Jarom 1:3*	0	0	0	1	0	0	0	0	0	0	0	0	1
great mercy	*Jacob 4:10*	0	0	1	0	0	0	2	0	0	0	0	0	3
greatness of the mercy	*2 Nephi 9:19*	0	1	0	0	0	0	0	0	0	0	0	0	1
infinite mercy	*Mosiah 28:4*	0	0	0	0	0	1	0	0	0	0	0	0	1
mercies	*2 Nephi 1:2*	0	2	0	0	0	0	3	0	1	1	0	2	9
merciful	*1 Nephi 1:14*	5	7	2	0	0	1	15	3	1	1	4	1	40
multitude of his tender mercies	*1 Nephi 8:8*	1	0	0	0	0	0	0	0	0	0	1	0	2
pure mercies	*Moroni 8:19*	0	0	0	0	0	0	0	0	0	0	0	1	1
tender mercies	*1 Nephi 1:20*	1	0	0	0	0	0	0	0	0	0	0	0	1
														117

God possesses passions: Loving attributes
Specific verse

	Category total	Line total	Moroni	Ether	Mormon	4 Nephi	3 Nephi	Helaman	Alma	Mosiah	Words of Mormon	Omni	Jarom	Enos	Jacob	2 Nephi	1 Nephi
Patience *Mosiah 4:6*		3	0	0	0	0	0	0	2	1	0	0	0	0	0	0	0
long-suffering *Mosiah 4:11*	12	9	1	0	1	0	0	0	5	2	0	0	0	0	0	0	0
TOTALS		221	14	12	7	1	9	8	71	29	0	0	1	0	13	34	22

God possesses passions: Judgmental attributes
Specific verse

	Category total	Line total	Moroni	Ether	Mormon	4 Nephi	3 Nephi	Helaman	Alma	Mosiah	Words of Mormon	Omni	Jarom	Enos	Jacob	2 Nephi	1 Nephi
Anger *1 Nephi 20:9*		19	0	2	0	0	0	0	2	2	0	0	0	0	1	11	1
angry *1 Nephi 18:10*		4	0	0	0	0	0	0	2	0	0	0	0	0	0	1	1
fierce anger *2 Nephi 23:9*		8	0	0	0	0	0	0	5	1	0	0	0	0	0	2	0
fiery indignation *Alma 40:14*		1	0	0	0	0	0	1	1	0	0	0	0	0	0	0	0

Word / Reference													5		34
fury — 2 Nephi 8:20	0	2	0	0	0	0	0	0	0	0	0	0	0		2
Chasten — 1 Nephi 16:39	1	0	0	0	0	0	0	0	0	0	0	0	0		1
chastened — 1 Nephi 16:39	1	0	0	0	0	0	0	0	0	0	0	0	0		1
rebuke — 2 Nephi 8:20	0	3	0	0	0	0	0	0	0	0	0	0	0		3
Displeasure — 2 Nephi 1:22	0	1	0	0	0	0	1	0	0	0	0	0	0		2
anguish — Mosiah 3:7	0	0	0	0	0	0	1	0	0	0	0	0	0		1
grief — Mosiah 14:10	0	0	0	0	0	0	2	0	0	0	0	0	0		2
grieveth — Jacob 5:51	0	0	6	0	0	0	0	0	0	0	0	0	0		6
jealous — Mosiah 11:22	0	0	0	0	0	0	2	0	0	0	0	0	0		2
sorrows — Mosiah 14:3	0	0	0	0	0	0	1	0	0	0	0	0	0		1
suffer — Mosiah 8:20	0	0	0	0	0	0	1	0	0	0	0	0	0		1
suffereth — Alma 7:13	0	0	0	0	0	0	2	1	0	0	0	0	0		3
sufferings — Mosiah 18:2	0	0	0	0	0	0	1	0	0	0	0	0	0		1

God possesses passions: Judgmental attributes — Specific verse	Category total	Line total	Moroni	Ether	Mormon	4 Nephi	3 Nephi	Helaman	Alma	Mosiah	Words of Mormon	Omni	Jarom	Enos	Jacob	2 Nephi	1 Nephi
troubled *3 Nephi 17:14*		1	0	0	0	0	1	0	0	0	0	0	0	0	0	0	0
vengeance *Mormon 3:15*		2	0	0	2	0	0	0	0	0	0	0	0	0	0	0	0
wept *Jacob 5:41*	25	3	0	0	0	0	2	0	0	0	0	0	0	0	1	0	0
Wrath *1 Nephi 13:11*		21	0	2	0	0	0	0	6	1	0	0	0	0	1	5	6
almighty wrath *Alma 54:6*		1	0	0	0	0	0	0	1	0	0	0	0	0	0	0	0
cup of the wrath *Mosiah 3:26*		2	0	0	0	0	0	0	0	2	0	0	0	0	0	0	0
fulness of his wrath *1 Nephi 22:17*		7	0	5	0	0	0	0	0	0	0	0	0	0	0	1	1
fulness of my wrath *Ether 9:20*		1	0	1	0	0	0	0	0	0	0	0	0	0	0	0	0
fulness of the wrath *1 Nephi 22:16*	35	3	0	0	0	0	0	0	0	0	0	0	0	0	0	0	3
TOTALS		99	0	10	2	0	3	0	18	17	0	0	0	0	9	26	14

"WHERE YOUR TREASURE IS,
THERE WILL YOUR HEART BE ALSO"

Searching the Book of Mormon to find those who knew, who did, but who never became is not difficult. There are numerous examples of the "never being," for the holy text speaks not just of individuals but of whole civilizations that never became as he is.

The common denominator of these failing people was pride. Carnal pressures exerted on the prosperous resulted in pride, pressing the prideful to "lift up their heads in wickedness . . . to commit whoredoms" (Alma 30:18), pressing the adulterous to lasciviousness and uncontrolled passions (Alma 45:1–13), pressing the angry to avenging hatred (Mormon 3:9–11) and, finally, self-destruction. That self-destruction included apostasy and spiritual death.

Pride was always the first step toward self-destruction. Pride resulted in failure "to be," which ultimately meant failure "to have" the blessings of the gospel. Preventing pride from taking its creeping, parasitic grip on us requires surrounding ourselves with the armor of God, so that we will be protected from pride now and in the future.

Yet how is this possible? We, like most of the Book of Mormon people, live in a prosperous, prideful era, an era in which our worth is often measured by our material accumulations. Buy now, pay later, keep up with the Joneses or even the neighbor next door—all are common themes in twentieth-century society. To acquire material things in this world but not to pride in what we acquire becomes our challenge. If we indulge ourselves in personal accumulation, we deny ourselves the blessings of righteous living, of becoming as he is.

The Book of Mormon tells us clearly how prosperity affects us and how pride robs us of the humility we need to acquire Christlike attributes to enjoy a happy life. One of the primary evidences of the effect of prosperity on us is how our heart reacts to it. The heart, in symbolic reference to our affections and willpower, is frequently mentioned in the Book of Mormon as a barometer of mental reaction to material prosperity.

The word *heart* appears in 168 verses of the Book of

Mormon. In 53 of these appearances the heart described yields itself to God and is made to rejoice because of the purity of its intentions; however, this rejoicing occurs only after a great struggle in which the heart is "broken" and becomes receptive to God's commands. The process of "breaking" the heart is recorded in 57 verses of the book. In 53 of the verses, or 93 percent of the time, the heart successfully yields itself to God. In 4 of the verses, however, is evidence of Satan's victory over individuals and their civilization when they fail in the breaking process and "harden" their hearts toward righteousness, embracing in its place the material world.

These 4 verses, combined with 63 other verses about "hardened" hearts, suggest an eventual outcome for Lehi's family: Satan's narrow victory over the hearts through wealth. The heart, therefore, is both a witness to Satan's frequent triumph over the will of man and a barometer of the eventual fall of Lehi's family, whose sacred promise to "keep the commandments and prosper" became its curse as they chose to reject God.

Lehi's family allowed their hearts to be polluted by the love of riches. Phrases such as setting their "heart upon riches" (Mosiah 11:14) and being "uncircumcised" (2 Nephi 9:33) with "stubbornness" (Alma 32:16) and "wickedness" of heart (Alma 10:6) all evidence the continued indulgence of the descendants of Lehi in the pleasures of the material world. Yielding to this enticement of Satan, many of Lehi's family were quick to allow their hearts to harden (1 Nephi 7:8) and slow to remember the commandments of God (Helaman 12:5). Their hearts did not rejoice in the potential blessings of prosperity but became set, in an idolatrous way, "upon gold, and upon silver, and upon all manner of fine goods." (Alma 31:24.) Lehi's descendants therefore sold "themselves for naught." (2 Nephi 26:10.)

But like their illustrious forebear, Lehi, these descendants eventually left behind their prosperity and were forced to make a lengthy journey. Unlike Lehi, however, they did not journey with a promise to a chosen land, but journeyed instead into the state of damnation, for their hearts were witnesses to their own earthly crime against God.

Just as he deals with us, so did the Lord deal mercifully

with Lehi's family. The Book of Mormon records the methods by which he attempted to redeem the family from its miserable destination. The Lord most frequently employed two methods. One is "bearing down in pure testimony against them" (Alma 4:19); the other is sending armies to moderate the hardness of their hearts "and level them with the earth" (Alma 51:17). The most effective approach was the first, that of the prophets sharing their humble testimonies. Their sure conviction often evoked sincere, sorrowful repentance.

The descendants of Lehi who listened and responded positively to the testimony of prophets had their hearts "moved" (2 Nephi 17:2), and they "groane[d]" (2 Nephi 4:19), were "weighed down with sorrow" (2 Nephi 1:17), and "wept" (2 Nephi 4:26), being "pained" (1 Nephi 17:47). They "experienced lowliness" (Moroni 7:44), and their hearts "melted" (2 Nephi 23:7). All of these feelings were necessary in order for their hearts to become softened (1 Nephi 2:16) or broken (2 Nephi 2:7).

The descendants of Lehi who successfully overcame the idolatrous worship of possessions through this humbling process gratefully recognized a "sincere" (Mosiah 26:29) and a "mighty change" (Alma 5:12) within their hearts. With "fresh courage" (Alma 15:4) and "renewed energy" (Moroni 7:48) and a desire for "oneness with God" (2 Nephi 1:21), the descendants of Lehi gained priceless perspective on wealth and its role in life. Their hearts took delight, once again, in righteousness (2 Nephi 9:49), and they became "magnified" (2 Nephi 25:13), experienced "purity" (Jacob 2:10), and "swelled with thanksgiving" (Alma 37:37) for the laws of righteousness and for the promised prosperity written therein. This thanksgiving focused ultimately on the Lord, for their hearts had become holy once again. (Alma 37:36–37.)

Pride is one of Satan's primary vehicles for entering into our hearts. Pride may be viewed as another useful barometer of whether we are yielding our hearts to the enticements of Satan and choosing the works of darkness. (2 Nephi 26:10.)

The word *pride* is found in sixty verses of the Book of Mormon; the word *proud*, in fourteen. Of these seventy-four appearances, not one of them may be considered a righteous pride. Instead, the word is used throughout the Book of Mormon in a negative sense. It had to be stripped from the descendants of Lehi because with it in their hearts, they were "not prepared to meet God." (Alma 5:28.)

Pride is not easily hidden by the one who indulges in it. Jacob said to those who possess it, "[Ye] wear stiff necks and high heads because of the costliness of your apparel, and persecute your brethren because ye suppose that ye are better than they." (Jacob 2:13.) The proud descendants of Lehi lifted themselves up in pride, "despising others, turning their backs upon the needy and the naked and those who were hungry, and those who were athirst, and those who were sick and afflicted." (Alma 4:12.) They also caused "oppression to the poor, . . . smiting their humble brethren upon the cheek, making a mock of that which was sacred, denying the spirit of prophecy and of revelation." (Helaman 4:12.) Satan can easily tempt the proud "to seek for power, and authority, and riches, and the vain things of the world." (3 Nephi 6:15.)

All of these undesirable characteristics are results "of their exceeding riches, and their fine silks, and their fine-twined linen, and because of their many flocks and herds, and their gold and their silver, and all manner of precious things, which they had obtained by their industry." (Alma 4:6.) This self-seeking aggrandizement is one of Satan's primary holds upon the heart.

In contrast, the Lord's vehicle for entering into our hearts is humility. Being humble is in direct opposition to being lifted up, puffed up, and swollen in self-importance. To be humble, the descendants of Lehi literally had to descend into the depths, for "notwithstanding their riches, or their strength, or their posterity . . . they did humble themselves exceedingly before [God]." (Alma 62:49.)

Humility occurs thirteen times in the Book of Mormon. Seven references use the phrase "the depths" or "dust" of humility. *Humble* is found in forty-seven verses. In each of these references, being humble or possessing humility is a desired characteristic, even if it has been forced by poverty.

The humble are able to maintain their humility only if they "fast and pray oft, and . . . wax stronger and stronger in their humility, and firmer and firmer in the faith of Christ, unto the filling their souls with joy and consolation, yea, even to the purifying and the sanctification of their hearts, which sanctification cometh because of their yielding their hearts unto God." (Helaman 3:35.) They also are "baptized, . . . visited with fire and with the Holy Ghost, and [are recipients of] a remission of their sins." (3 Nephi 12:2.)

Humility, the gateway to sanctification, is not an easy path, for the proud "persecute the true church of Christ, because of their humility and their belief in Christ." (4 Nephi 1:29.) "Yea, they did persecute them, and afflict them with all manner of words, and this because of their humility; because they were not proud in their own eyes, and because they did impart the word of God, one with another, without money and without price." (Alma 1:20.) The Lord strengthens his humble people with renewed determination during difficult persecutions, which determination causes them to proclaim, "Yea, I will keep thy commandments with all my heart." (Alma 45:7.)

The humble descendants of Lehi in the Book of Mormon received the promise of prosperity to bless their lives, and they used their prosperity frequently to bless the lives of others. For example, Nephi used precious metals to inscribe sacred history for unborn generations. (1 Nephi 19:1.) King Benjamin counseled his people, "And ye will not suffer your children that they go hungry, or naked." (Mosiah 4:14.) "Ye will administer of your substance unto him that standeth in need; and ye will not suffer that the beggar putteth up his petition to you in vain." (Mosiah 4:16.) In essence, King Benjamin admonished his people to impart of their property gained in prosperity freely one to another. (Mosiah 4:21.)

These two examples illustrate what has been called the Golden Rule. "A new commandment I give unto you," Jesus said, "that ye love one another; as I have loved you, that ye also love one another." (John 13:34.) The observance of the Golden Rule is essential, particularly if we desire to continue to enjoy the Lord's promised prosperity.

Fourth Nephi describes the most prosperous events of the land of promise. "And they had all things common among them; therefore there were not rich and poor . . . and the Lord did prosper them exceedingly in the land." (4 Nephi 1:3, 7.) This prosperity led to the scriptural observation,

"Surely there could not be a happier people among all the people who had been created by the hand of God." (4 Nephi 1:16.)

The intriguing paradox that we must give of our material substance to truly enjoy it is in direct contrast to Satan's tactics of hoarding it, accumulating it, and becoming proud. The underlying principle of keeping the commandments and enjoying prosperity is plain: that which you freely give to bless the life of another will bless your own life. For example, after blessing five loaves of bread and two fishes, Christ fed five thousand men. After the meal he gathered twelve baskets full of fragments. What had originally appeared to be a meager offering to assist others turned into a feast. (Mark 6:40–43.) Lehi left his material wealth in Jerusalem, only for him and his posterity to acquire more goods in the land of promise.

True charity is important in order to learn how to experience a mighty change in our heart. First, we need to know about the Savior and his teachings, which lead us to eternal life. Second, we need to do or apply his teachings in our day-to-day living. Third, and most important, we need to be even as he is.

He is caring, loving, nurturing, and forgiving. He is constant. He is the God of Abraham, Isaac, and Jacob. He is a living God who possesses body parts and passions. He uses them to strengthen, bless, and encourage each of us. He sets the exemplary pattern; even during times when we are not as valiant, the Lord shows forth abundant offers of mercy and comfort and gives us the loving guidance of valiant prophets. Unfortunately, despite his certain, clarion call, most of the Book of Mormon people chose to reject him and his teachings. Their hearts became hardened to righteous principles. Humility gave way under the pressures of prosperous pride. Our challenge, like the challenge of Lehi's extended family, is to live in a world of prosperous circumstances, yet to keep our eye single to his glory—to look to the Savior as the Supreme Being, the Great I Am.

Chapter 5

NOT WITHOUT HOPE

Press forward with a steadfastness in Christ,
having a perfect brightness of hope, and
a love of God and of all men.
2 Nephi 31:20

The fact that most ancient Americans again and again rejected the word of God may lead us to conclude that the Book of Mormon is little more than a methodical course in spiritual failure. The pattern is evident in the apostate lives of King Noah, Gadianton, Nehor, and the masses who followed their satanic examples. Their love of riches, rebellion against God, and embracing of Satan's enticements leaves us with a sense of solemn foreboding, even forewarning, of what the future may bring. Yet there is within the Book of Mormon a contrasting message of hope. We must not forget that in the description of every apostate there is a righteous exemplar: for a Korihor, an Alma; for a Sherem, a Jacob; and for an Amalickiah, a Captain Moroni. The Book of Mormon not only clearly defines the broad path to spiritual and material ruin but also, through the example of Christ and the righteous minority, defines the narrow path, the iron rod, that leads to spiritual well-being. Failure and its recurring ills result from the choice not to keep the commandments of God. Success and bright hope stem from obedient adherence to those commandments.

Just as there were valiant Saints in ancient America, so today there are many who have chosen to keep the commandments despite the majority's choice not to. The parable of the good Samaritan is exemplified now, as then, by these modern Saints. For example, my Sunday School class

71

recently showed a Christlike love to Virginia Nibley, a child with Down's syndrome. In class, Virginia whispered to me that she wanted to sing "The First Noel." I agreed, knowing it wasn't close to Christmas and wondering if that would cause the other children to make fun of her.

With trepidation I announced in class, "Virginia wants to sing a Christmas solo." To my surprise, no one laughed. Virginia sang from memory the first five stanzas. Then there was the unforgettable moment of awkward silence as she struggled, then failed, to recall the next phrase.

We all knew what the next stanza was but hesitated to interject. The awkward silence continued. Virginia began to cry. Where was a happy resolution to the uncomfortable silence?

Without prompting, one young classmate started singing "The First Noel" from the beginning. Virginia smiled and joined in. Then not only did Virginia sing but the entire class sang.

These good Samaritans quietly lifted the load of the despondent and the despairing. To the least within their midst they gave hope. They, like the valiant minority of Book of Mormon men, women, and children, have faith in the teachings of Jesus Christ. They are becoming even as he is.

Examples of Christlike behavior inspire us to rise up from the world's rejection of the Savior's teachings and join the elect few who keep the commandments, hold to the iron rod, and persevere. These elect few we call Saints, whether they live in our time or in the time of the ancient American prophets.

A multitude of such individuals were so spiritually purified and had their lives so changed that they could see the resurrected Lord in America. A few individuals saw the Savior at other significant times. (Alma 19:29.) But only twenty-two men are referred to by name in the Book of Mormon as having seen the Son of God: the brother of Jared (Ether 3:15), King Emer (Ether 9:22), Ether (Ether 13:4), Lehi (1 Nephi 1:8–9), Nephi (1 Nephi 11:1), Jacob (2 Nephi 2:4), King Lamoni (Alma 19:13), Alma (Alma 36:22), Mormon (Mormon 1:15), Moroni (Ether 12:39), Nephi (brother to Timothy), Timothy, Jonas, Mathoni, Mathonihah, Kumen,

Kumenonhi, Jeremiah, Shemnon, Jonas, Zedekiah, and Isaiah (3 Nephi 19:4). Of the twenty-two, three were Jaredites and nineteen were descendants of Lehi.

There are four instructive parallels between Christ's separate appearances to the three Jaredites and to the nineteen members of Lehi's family. First, the founders of each civilization saw Christ before arriving in the promised land: the brother of Jared (Ether 3:6–15) and Lehi (1 Nephi 1:8–9). Second, a king within each culture was privileged to see the Lord Jesus: Emer (Ether 9:22) and Lamoni (Alma 19:13). Third, the last known prophet of each fallen civilization received a manifestation: Moroni (Ether 12:39) and Ether (Ether 13:4). Fourth, within both cultures throngs saw the Lord: the Jaredites (Ether 12:19) and the multitude at the temple in the land of Bountiful (3 Nephi 11:16–17).

These manifestations indicate the great faith and righteousness of these people, because they are the fulfillment of the Lord's promise "that he manifesteth himself unto all those who believe in him, by the power of the Holy Ghost; yea, unto every nation, kindred, tongue, and people, working mighty miracles, signs, and wonders, among the children of men according to their faith." (2 Nephi 26:13.)

Many individuals could be classified as members of the most righteous and faithful minority who were worthy to know through a visual manifestation that Jesus is the Christ. To them we add that multitude of unnamed righteous followers who knew, not by sight, but through the gift of faith, that Jesus is the Christ. We thus begin to realize the substantial size of the minority.

Helaman epitomized the faithful follower's belief in the divine sonship of Jesus: "Believest thou in Jesus Christ, who shall come?" Alma asked Helaman. "And he said, Yea, I believe all the words which thou hast spoken." (Alma 45:4–5.) This theme occurs over and over again as the faithful Saints sought to be faithful to their beliefs and to know of the truthfulness of Christ's message. Helaman represented not a small group but a host of faithful Saints whose number is unknown. For example, from 90 B.C. to 65 B.C., thousands of Lamanites believed the gospel as taught by the four sons of Mosiah, and they never faltered in their testimony of Christ. (Alma 23:6.) The Lamanites proved valiant, and they reared two thousand sons, whose faith in God and his power of deliverance was so strong that "not one soul of them [did fall] to the earth" (Alma 56:56) while they fought for the cause of liberty.

Even though the number in this faithful group is unknown, the nobility of their actions is apparent. They, like their prophetic leaders, sought to declare the word of God. (Mosiah 3:13.) Through the words of God they brought peace to a war-torn land. (Words of Mormon 1:18.) They exhorted the majority to be faithful and to repent of their sins. (Helaman 6:4.) They testified boldly concerning the redemption of the Lord. (3 Nephi 6:20.)

They, like their prophets, endured suffering and persecution for their beliefs. Faithful members of the Church had "persecution which was heaped upon them." (Alma 1:25.) Such persecution was prevalent in both the Jaredite and the Nephite cultures. In the Jaredite culture, "the people believed not the words of the prophets, but they cast them out; and some of them they cast into pits and left them to perish." (Ether 9:29.) In the Nephite culture, many who testified boldly of Christ "were taken and put to death secretly by the judges." (3 Nephi 6:23.) Alma and Amulek witnessed women and children being cast into the fire to meet a martyr's fate because of their belief in Jesus Christ. (Alma 14:8–9.)

The integrity and endurance of the collective faithful are made known in the Book of Mormon; yet their individual names do not appear. One reason may be that the purpose of the Book of Mormon is to convince "the Jew and Gentile that Jesus is the Christ, the Eternal God" (title page of the Book of Mormon), not to list the names of the faithful. This reasoning is consistent with Nephi's stated desire not to encumber the metal plates with genealogies. (1 Nephi 6.) Perhaps when we have other records of these two cultures, we will find lists of the valiant. In the meantime, it is a privilege for us to name twenty-two who were worthy to see Jesus the Christ, the Son of an Eternal God.

The Lord's prophets gathered these believers and many more from the ranks of the unbelievers. Jacob recorded, "We did magnify our office unto the Lord, taking upon us the responsibility" of teaching the word of God and the need for repentance to the people. (Jacob 1:19; 2:2.) This twofold assignment was consistently magnified by holy prophets in the Book of Mormon as they gathered the believers in Christ.

The prophets taught the word of God to the people through inspired utterances that pertained to the past (2 Nephi 2:25), to the present (Alma 18:16), and to the future (1 Nephi 1:18) and dealt most frequently with the Savior. Other prophecies were warnings (Mosiah 12) or new truths that had been revealed (Helaman 8:27).

If the people understood and accepted the word of God, or prophecy, as taught by the holy prophets, they desired to repent of their sins and live better lives. (Mosiah 5:2.) Most often, the prophets encountered people whose hearts had become hardened and who did not want to repent; as a result, the people rejected the prophets' cry for repentance. Yet Alma, amid trials and afflictions in calling his people to repentance, expressed his love for this assignment: "O that I were an angel, and could have the wish of mine heart, that I might go forth and speak with the trump of God, with a voice to shake the earth, and cry repentance unto every people!" (Alma 29:1.)

Alma may have desired to cry repentance to so many because in this work of great charity, he could plant in the hearts of the people the seed that, if nourished, would grow to eternal life. (Alma 32.) Similar feelings may have motivated the prophet Ether, who "did cry from the morning, even until the going down of the sun, exhorting the people to believe in God unto repentance." (Ether 12:3.)

When the prophets cried repentance, their words left no doubt about their meaning. Nephi proclaimed, "O ye fools, ye uncircumcised of heart, ye blind, and ye stiffnecked people." (Helaman 9:21.) Samuel the Lamanite shouted from the walls of the Nephite city of Zarahemla, "O ye wicked and ye perverse generation; ye hardened and ye stiffnecked people, how long will ye suppose that the Lord will suffer you?" (Helaman 13:29.)

The meaning of the cry of repentance was clear, but the reception of it was mixed. The prophetic cries brought individuals to a knowledge of salvation and multitudes to their knees. (Helaman 6:4-6.) But most often the prophets' cry went unheeded, and they saw the word of God trampled by the vices of the people. (Helaman 7:3; Ether 13:2, 13.) Yet these noble prophets continued to proclaim the word with soberness all their days. Why were they so bold in their declarations? They wanted the people to know the freedom of casting off the burden of guilt and becoming clean from sin. They knew that repentance is essential to salvation and that without it no accountable person can be saved in the kingdom of God. (Mosiah 17:10–11.) In essence, it was their desire to be obedient and fulfill faithfully their calling as prophets of the Most High God in gathering the elect from the ranks of the unbelievers. (Alma 36:3.)

Prophets of God display deep sensitivity when the word of God is rejected, and they sorrow that those who reject Christ will ultimately be rejected by him. The prophets in the Book of Mormon are no exception. Nephi was often grieved by the hardness of the hearts of his family members. (1 Nephi 7:8.) Jacob told the people, "I this day am weighed down with much more desire and anxiety for the welfare of your souls than I have hitherto been." (Jacob 2:3.) Iniquity among the people was the cause of great sorrow to Alma. (Alma 31:2.) Mormon cried, "And wo is me because of their wickedness; for my heart has been filled with sorrow because of their wickedness, all my days." (Mormon 2:19.) Even the three disciples who tarried from the days of Jesus "began to sorrow for the sins of the world." (4 Nephi 1:44.)

Many prophets in the Book of Mormon grieved over the people's rejection of the word of God. Their sorrow was often accompanied by persecution. From 600 B.C. when the people of Jerusalem sought to take Lehi's life (1 Nephi 1:19–20) to A.D. 421 when Moroni faced destruction by the Lamanites (Moroni 1:1), persecution was the lot and the heritage of prophets and the faithful minority in America.

Like Christ, who endured scourging, mockery, thorns, and death, his prophets and his Saints endured similar mistreatment. Nephi fled from his plotting brothers. (2 Nephi 5:1–4.) Alma and Amulek endured prison. (Alma 14:22.) Ether dwelt in the cavity of a rock. (Ether 13:18.) Abinadi suffered death by fire. (Mosiah 17:20.) They endured such extreme hardship, suffering, and persecution because they would not deny their words: "I will not recall the words which I have spoken unto you concerning this people, for they are true; and that ye may know of their surety I have suffered myself that I have fallen into your hands. Yea, and I will suffer even until death, and I will not recall my words, and they shall stand as a testimony against you." (Mosiah 17:9–10.)

Amid extreme mocking, anger, gnashing of teeth, and persecution, one truth is poignantly clear: The Lord will not leave his devoted followers comfortless. In affliction, persecution, and suffering, the Lord sends heavenly aid.

Just as God the Father comforted his Son, so he will comfort us when we are valiant amid persecution. Again, the Book of Mormon Saints taught us how the Lord shows his love in times of trials. Sorrow eventually becomes glory. Persecution proves a crown of righteousness. Heavenly strength does come to those worthy prophets and the faithful minority who do not fear persecution but seek to do the will of God and keep his commandments. (Helaman 10:4.)

The Book of Mormon illustrates at least three forms of heavenly strength that can come in the midst of sorrow and persecution:

The Lord sends angels to minister to his people. An angel intervened when Nephi was smitten by a rod at the hands of his elder brothers. (1 Nephi 3:28–30.) Jacob was ministered to by angels while contending with Sherem about the truthfulness of Christ. (Jacob 7:5.) Alma was "weighed down with sorrow, wading through much tribulation and anguish of soul, because of the wickedness of the people" when "an angel of the Lord appeared unto him, saying: Blessed art thou, Alma." (Alma 8:14–15.) While Lehi and Nephi were in prison, they "were encircled about as if by fire" (Helaman 5:23), and they conversed with the angels of God (Helaman 5:39). In the case of a sorrowful, dejected Nephi, "angels did minister unto him daily." (3 Nephi 7:18.)

The Lord delivers the faithful from persecution. Mosiah was warned by the Lord that he should flee out of the land of Nephi. (Omni 1:12.) The Lord delivered Abinadi from his enemies when his life was threatened. (Mosiah 11:26.) Alma and Amulek could not be confined in dungeons or slain because the Lord delivered them from their enemies. (Alma 8:31; 14:26–27; 36:27.) Helaman received assurance of the deliverance of his two thousand sons from the threat of death. (Alma 58:11.) Nephi was given such power that his enemies could not cast him into prison, "for he was taken by the Spirit and conveyed away out of the midst of them." (Helaman 10:16.)

The Lord preserves his people during persecution. Nephi wrote, "My God hath been my support; he hath led me through mine afflictions in the wilderness; and he hath preserved me upon the waters of the great deep." (2 Nephi 4:20.) The Lord preserved Abinadi when the king wanted him slain. (Mosiah 13:3.) The Lord strengthened the people of Alma "that they could bear up their burdens with ease, and they did submit cheerfully and with patience to all the will of the Lord." (Mosiah 24:15.) The Lord watched over his servants in the land of the apostate Zoramites. (Alma 31:38.) Samuel was not hit by stones and arrows while he stood on the wall of Zarahemla because of the preserving power of God. (Helaman 16:2.)

The faithful in the Book of Mormon were tested and tried in their ability to do the will of God and keep his commandments. Each prophet magnified his calling and proclaimed to his people the word of Christ and the charitable cry of repentance. As a result of faithful fulfillment of their assignments, many prophets — and those they converted — had to endure loneliness, affliction, sorrow, and persecution. Amid these difficult conditions, the faithful minority received heavenly strength to endure their trials. Instead of renouncing God for the afflictions they endured, they loved and worshipped him. They showed us how to live as Christ lived — enduring all things in love.

The names of only a few of the righteous are recorded in the Book of Mormon. Their consistent faithfulness earned for them an assurance of eternal life. Lehi's parting words indicate his knowledge of his eternal reward: "The Lord hath redeemed my soul from hell; I have beheld his glory, and I am encircled about eternally in the arms of his love." (2 Nephi 1:15.) Nephi rejoiced, "I glory in my Jesus, for he hath redeemed my soul from hell." (2 Nephi 33:6.) Enos, toward the end of his life, wrote, "I soon go to the place of my rest, which is with my Redeemer; for I know that in him I shall rest." (Enos 1:27.) Alma affirmed, "I know that he will raise me up at the last day, to dwell with him in glory." (Alma 36:28.)

We too will have opportunity to know with assurance that these noble prophets received eternal life, for we will meet them before the bar of God. Nephi assured us that "you and I shall stand face to face before his bar." (2 Nephi 33:11.) Jacob bade us farewell "until I shall meet you before the pleasing bar of God." (Jacob 6:13.) Moroni also wrote, "Ye shall see me at the bar of God." (Moroni 10:27.) Then the mockers, the persecutors, and the blasphemers will know that these holy men who lived in America were indeed prophets of God.

CONCLUSION

The lives as well as the words of the valiant few are witnesses of Christ. We learn from their example what it means to be as Christ is. The faithful minority in each generation has clearly defined the path for success: keeping the commandments of God. The faithful in the Book of Mormon clung tenaciously to this concept amid persecution, affliction, sorrow, and threatening death. Their lives epitomize the results of a secure grasp on the rod of iron, the word of God.

The example of the faithful minority is worthy of our emulation. Their devotion, love for God, and integrity provide a course for daily living. In that course is the remembrance that the minority had the potential to become the majority. If more people had let their hearts be softened, the majority would have known the goodness of God.

"Wherefore, ye must press forward with a steadfastness in Christ, having a perfect brightness of hope, and a love of God and of all men. Wherefore, if ye shall press forward, feasting upon the word of Christ, and endure to the end, behold, thus saith the Father: Ye shall have eternal life." (2 Nephi 31:20.)

Chapter 6

A TESTIMONY OF JOSEPH, A WITNESS OF CHRIST

The Book of Mormon [is] the most correct
of any book on earth, and the keystone
of our religion, and a man would get
nearer to God by abiding by its precepts,
than by any other book.
Joseph Smith

The earth has yielded up its treasure known to all faithful members of The Church of Jesus Christ of Latter-day Saints as "a marvellous work and a wonder." (Isaiah 29:14.) The long-awaited stick of Joseph has come forth by the power of God as a second witness for Jesus Christ. Records laboriously inscribed on metal plates by prophetic scribes have now been revealed. The doctrinal restoration has commenced with a profound and powerful witness for Christ, the Book of Mormon.

The very existence of the Book of Mormon testifies that Joseph Smith was a translator of God's words. As in the pattern of all prophets of old, Joseph's life as well as his words taught us how to be as Christ is. Joseph's life paralleled the lives of earlier prophets in the western hemisphere.

While yet in his youth Joseph Smith was privileged to see Christ. Like the twenty-two men named in the Book of Mormon who saw Christ, he left his testimony of the Savior's appearance to him. Speaking of the clear spring morning of 1820 when he went into the woods in western New York to pray, Joseph recorded the following:

"When the light rested upon me I saw two Personages, whose brightness and glory defy all description, standing above me in the air. One of them spake unto me, calling me by name and said, pointing to the other—*This is My Beloved Son. Hear Him!*" (Joseph Smith–History 1:17.)

On February 16, 1832, at Hiram, Ohio, while Joseph engaged in studious, prayerful consideration of the things of heaven with Sidney Rigdon, they "beheld the glory of the Son, on the right hand of the Father, and received of his fulness." (D&C 76:20.) On Sunday, April 3, 1836, Joseph and Oliver Cowdery retired to the pulpit of the Kirtland Temple to pray silently. Once again the glorious, resurrected Savior appeared. (George A. Smith, in *Journal of Discourses*, 11:10; Hyrum M. Smith and Janne E. Sjodahl, *The Doctrine and Covenants Commentary*, p. 724; Malachi 3:1.)

Like the prophets of ancient America, Joseph Smith gathered around him a multitude who knew by faith, not by sight, that Jesus is the Christ. The names of many of these faithful Saints are not known. What is known is their faithfulness under adverse circumstances. An extermination order, the Haun's Mill Massacre, the Battle of Crooked River, and the exodus to the West are only phrases. Yet the recitation of them brings to mind persecution, affliction, and death endured by unnumbered and unnamed valiant Saints.

Joseph Smith, like the ancient prophets, magnified the callings he had received. As a prophet, seer, revelator, and translator, Joseph bore strong responsibility from the Lord. He fulfilled many divine charges. Two of these responsibilities were to prophesy (D&C 21:5) and to cry repentance (D&C 6:9), just as did those righteous prophets who preceded him. The Doctrine and Covenants is filled with sacred prophecies given to Joseph pertaining to the past, the present, and the future. (D&C 1:37–39; 11:25; 21:4–5; Articles of Faith 1:7.) Likewise, the Doctrine and Covenants is a repository of the cry of repentance. (D&C 1:27; 6:9; 11:9; 16:6; 42:24–28; 133:16; Articles of Faith 1:4.) Joseph Smith taught, "We believe in preaching the doctrine of repentance in all the world." (*Teachings of the Prophet Joseph Smith*, p. 82.)

Like those of the ancient prophets, Joseph's cry of repentance and his prophetic utterances had a mixed reception. Only the righteous heeded. (D&C 18:13.) The majority rejected both Joseph Smith and the word of the Lord. In the wake of rejection came Joseph's continual foe — persecution. Ridicule, arrest warrants, and evil speaking were his common companions. Enemies, mobbers, and traitors sought to thwart the plan of God. Doctrines Joseph held sacred, such as plural marriage, temple ordinances, and the nature of God, were distorted by apostates to disprove his claims of divine revelation and to arouse public sentiment against him. Persecution stalked the Prophet from the spring of 1820 until his martyrdom in 1844.

Yet amid the persecution, suffering, rejection, and loneliness, the Lord did not leave Joseph comfortless. Like the prophets of the Book of Mormon, Joseph conversed with angels. (Joseph Smith–History 1:30.) While in Liberty Jail under the sentence of death, the Prophet was promised that he would be delivered and his friends would greet him again "with warm hearts and friendly hands." (D&C 121:9.) Joseph spoke to his fellow prisoners confidently about the preserving power of God that would be exercised in their behalf: "Be of good cheer, brethren; the word of the Lord came to me last night that our lives should be given us, and that whatever we may suffer during this captivity, not one of our lives should be taken." (As quoted by Parley P. Pratt, *Autobiography of Parley Parker Pratt*, p. 192.) Joseph and his associates were spared, as prophesied.

It was not until June 27, 1844, that Joseph's life was taken at Carthage. For Joseph Smith, Carthage was a scene of broken promises, oaths of conspiracy, illegal arraignment, and fatal incarceration. Accusations of riot were turned to accusations of treason. Rumors once whispered were now shouted. The throngs unabashedly declared that Joseph would not leave Carthage alive. The Warsaw mobs sang, "Where now is the Prophet Joseph? Where now is the Prophet Joseph? Where now is the Prophet Joseph? Safe in Carthage jail!" (B. H. Roberts, *A Comprehensive History of The Church of Jesus Christ of Latter-day Saints*, 2:281.) Even the governor, though not in boisterous song, joined with the chorus of conspirators, mobbers, and militia in abetting the deaths of Joseph and his brother Hyrum.

Unwittingly, the assassins left behind much more than the corpses of two men. They left "a broad seal affixed to 'Mormonism' that cannot be rejected by any court on earth." They left "truth of the everlasting gospel that all the world cannot impeach." (D&C 135:7.) They left two martyr's crowns, which they helped forge with their senseless brutality. The testifiers are dead; yet their testament lives on. Joseph's seal is affixed to the truthfulness of the Book of Mormon as another witness for Jesus Christ. Throughout eternity Joseph will be numbered with the sanctified and the religious martyrs of all ages.

Joseph Smith was a prophet of God who, like Nephi, Jacob, and Moroni, saw Jesus Christ. He, like Alma and Lehi, prophesied the words of God and cried repentance to the people. As Mormon and Ether were persecuted for their testimony of the Lord, so too was Joseph. As Abinadi suffered a martyr's fate, so too did Joseph, to seal his testimony. He had faithfully and progressively forged this testimony from his youthful utterance in the Palmyra woods to his manly cry at Carthage. Like Jacob, Moroni, and Nephi, Joseph Smith, whose testimony and obedience were the continuum of his life's labors, knew his standing before God: "For I am the Lord thy God, and will be with thee even unto the end of the world, and through all eternity; for verily I seal upon you your exaltation, and prepare a throne for you in the kingdom of my Father, with Abraham your father." (D&C 132:49.)

To the thorough, prayerful reader the very existence of the Book of Mormon is an irrefutable testimony that Joseph Smith was a prophet and translator of God. The contents of the book are an irrefutable testament that Jesus Christ is the Son of God. He is clearly the central focus of the Book of Mormon. The Book of Mormon was preserved to come forth in these latter days to convince the "Jew and Gentile [through its contents] that Jesus is the Christ, the Eternal God." (Title page of the Book of Mormon.) Its purpose is to verify the divine sonship of the Nazarene to those who "ask with a sincere heart, with real intent, having faith in Christ." (Moroni 10:4.)

If we seek, we will find the Book of Mormon writers focused on the Savior. These ancient prophetic scribes had a conviction of the divinity of Jesus, for they knew him. Christ was revealed to the ancient prophets by the power of the Holy Ghost. And by the power of the Holy Ghost they wrote this second witness of Jesus Christ, the Book of Mormon.

Through the faithful efforts of the prophets and through divine intervention, the promised stick of Joseph, known in latter days as the Book of Mormon, has come forth: "Behold, I will take the stick of Joseph [the Book of Mormon], which is in the hand of Ephraim, and the tribes of Israel his fellows, and will put them with him, even with the stick of Judah [the Bible], and make them one stick, and they shall be one in mine hand." (Ezekiel 37:19.) It was translated by a seer chosen "to bring forth my word . . . and not to the bringing forth my word only, saith the Lord, but to the convincing them of my word, which shall have already gone forth among them." (2 Nephi 3:11.)

The most profound testimony of the Book of Mormon was given by the Lord Jesus Christ: "He [Joseph Smith] has translated the book, even that part which I have commanded him, and as your Lord and your God liveth it is true." (D&C 17:6.) The Lord's unequivocal statement is supported by Joseph Smith's own testimony of the coming forth of the Book of Mormon. (Introduction to the Book of Mormon.) These testimonies are convincing evidence of the truth of this "marvellous work and a wonder." (Isaiah 29:14.)

The Lord provided eleven others to see the gold plates and be special witnesses of the divinity of the Book of Mormon. Three of these eleven witnesses wrote the following: "Be it known unto all nations, kindreds, tongues, and people, unto whom this work shall come: That we, through the grace of God the Father, and our Lord Jesus Christ, have seen the plates which contain this record. . . . And we also know that they have been translated by the gift and power of God, for his voice hath declared it unto us; wherefore we know of a surety that the work is true." (Oliver Cowdery, David Whitmer, and Martin Harris, The Testimony of Three Witnesses, in Introduction to the Book of Mormon.)

Eight of the eleven witnesses wrote this statement:

"Be it known unto all nations, kindreds, tongues, and people, unto whom this work shall come: That Joseph

Smith, Jun., the translator of this work, has shown unto us the plates . . . ; and as many of the leaves as the said Smith has translated we did handle with our hands. . . . And we lie not, God bearing witness of it." (Christian Whitmer, Jacob Whitmer, Peter Whitmer, Jun., John Whitmer, Hiram Page, Joseph Smith, Sen., Hyrum Smith, and Samuel H. Smith, The Testimony of Eight Witnesses, in Introduction to the Book of Mormon.)

Each prophet in the dispensation of the fulness of times has testified of the truthfulness of the Book of Mormon. The following are a few examples of their testimony of this ancient holy text and their love for it.

Joseph Smith, Jr. (1805–1844). "The Book of Mormon [is] the most correct of any book on earth, and the keystone of our religion, and a man would get nearer to God by abiding by its precepts, than by any other book." (*Teachings of the Prophet Joseph Smith*, p. 194.)

Brigham Young (1801–1877). "When the book of Mormon was first printed, it came to my hands in two or three weeks afterwards. . . .

"I examined the matter studiously for two years before I made up my mind to receive that book. I knew it was true, as well as I knew that I could see with my eyes, or feel by the touch of my fingers, or be sensible of the demonstration of any sense. Had not this been the case, I never would have embraced it to this day." (In *Journal of Discourses*, 3:91.)

John Taylor (1808–1887). "The Gospel in the Book of Mormon and the Gospel in the Bible both agree: the doctrines in both books are one. The historical part differs only: the one gives the history of an Asiatic, the other of an American people. . . .

". . . it is true, and we know it." (In *Journal of Discourses*, 5:240–41.)

Wilford Woodruff (1807–1898). "As I did so [began to read the Book of Mormon] the spirit bore witness that the record which it contained was true. I opened my eyes to see, my ears to hear, and my heart to understand. I also opened my doors to entertain the servants of God." (Matthias F. Cowley, *Wilford Woodruff*, p. 34.)

Lorenzo Snow (1814–1901). "I had an intimate acquaintance with Joseph Smith, the Prophet, for a number of years. The position he occupied before the world and the declarations which he made were of an extraordinary character. It was a position which no individual before or since has attempted to assume. I know Joseph Smith to have been an honest man, a man of truth, honor, and fidelity, willing to sacrifice everything he possessed, even life itself, as a testimony to the heavens and the world that he had borne the truth to the human family." (*The Teachings of Lorenzo Snow*, pp. 56–57.)

On another occasion President Snow testified: "Joseph Smith declared that an angel from heaven revealed to him the golden plates of the Book of Mormon." (*The Teachings of Lorenzo Snow*, p. 57.)

Joseph F. Smith (1838–1918). "It cannot be disproved, for it is true. There is not a word of doctrine, of admonition, of instruction within its lids, but what agrees in sentiment and veracity with those of Christ and His Apostles, as contained in the Bible. Neither is there a word of counsel, of admonition or reproof within its lids, but what is calculated to make a bad man a good man, and a good man a better man, if he will hearken to it. It bears the mark of inspiration from beginning to end, and carries conviction to every honest-hearted soul." (In *Journal of Discourses*, 25:99–100.)

Heber J. Grant (1856–1945). "The Book of Mormon is in absolute harmony from start to finish with other sacred scriptures. There is not a doctrine taught in it that does not harmonize with the teachings of Jesus Christ. There is not one single expression in the Book of Mormon that would wound in the slightest degree the sensitiveness of any individual. There is not a thing in it but what is for the benefit and uplift of mankind. It is in every way a true witness for God, and it sustains the Bible and is in harmony with the Bible." (In Conference Report, Apr. 1929, pp. 128–29.)

George Albert Smith (1870–1951). "It fills my heart with joy to know that every man who will read it prayerfully, every man who will desire to know whether it be of God or not has the promise, not of Joseph Smith or any living human being, but the promise of our Heavenly Father that they shall know of a surety that it is of God. (Moroni 10:3–4–5). . . .

". . . These two books [the Book of Mormon and the

Bible] hand in hand teach us all where we came from, why we are here, where we may go, and they both contain the advice, the loving advice of our Heavenly Father intended to inspire us to do that which will enrich our lives here and prepare us for eternal happiness." (In Conference Report, Apr. 1936, pp. 15–16.)

David O. McKay (1873–1970). "I know that the gospel was restored through the Prophet Joseph Smith, by the Father and the Son, who are as real today in connection with the other world as my loved ones and yours." (*Gospel Ideals*, p. 85.)

On a later occasion President McKay said: "It [the Book of Mormon] is a physical fact, a sensible fact, there were witnesses to it, the reliability of those witnesses is established, there are monuments and memorials to it, and those monuments and memorials date back to the event itself." (*Gospel Ideals*, p. 87.)

Joseph Fielding Smith (1876–1972). "I want to bear testimony to you . . . that I know that the Book of Mormon is true; that Joseph Smith received it from the hand of God through an angel that was sent to reveal it, the same angel who, while living in this world, finished the record and sealed it up to come forth in this Dispensation of the Fulness of Times." (*Improvement Era*, Dec. 1961, p. 926.)

Harold B. Lee (1899–1973). "By this second witness we may know more certainly the meaning of the teachings of the ancient prophets and, indeed, of the Master and His disciples as they lived and taught among men. This should inspire all who would be honest seekers after truth to put these two sacred scriptures together and study them as one book, understanding, as we do, their true relationship." (*Ye Are the Light of the World*, p. 91.)

Spencer W. Kimball (1895–1985). "It is the word of God. It is a powerful second witness of Christ. . . .

"In the final chapter of the book is the never-failing promise that every person who will read the book with a sincere, prayerful desire to know of its divinity shall have the assurance. . . .

"My beloved friends, I give to you the Book of Mormon. May you read it prayerfully, study it carefully, and receive for yourselves the testimony of its divinity." (*Improvement Era*, June 1963, pp. 493–95.)

Ezra Taft Benson (1899–   ). "The Book of Mormon is the keystone in our witness of Jesus Christ, who is Himself the cornerstone of everything we do. It bears witness of His reality with power and clarity. Unlike the Bible, which passed through generations of copyists, translators, and corrupt religionists who tampered with the text, the Book of Mormon came from writer to reader in just one inspired step of translation. Therefore, its testimony of the Master is clear, undiluted, and full of power. . . . Truly, this divinely inspired book is a keystone in bearing witness to the world that Jesus is the Christ (see title page of the Book of Mormon)." (In Conference Report, Oct. 1986, p. 4; or *Ensign*, Nov. 1986, p. 5.)

Christ testified. Joseph testified. Eleven witnesses testified. Each prophet in this dispensation testified. Each of them knew the Book of Mormon was the word of God. Each knew that metal plates and interpreters had been preserved to come forth in the latter days to our generation. Each knew that this "marvellous work and a wonder" (Isaiah 29:14) was translated by the Prophet Joseph Smith.

After all the testimonies written and spoken of the Book of Mormon, the key question is, What do you think of the book? "Either the Book of Mormon is true, or it is false; either it came from God, or it was spawned in the infernal realms. It declares plainly that all men must accept it as pure scripture or they will lose their souls. It is not and cannot be simply another treatise on religion; it either came from heaven or from hell. And it is time for all those who seek salvation to find out for themselves whether it is of the Lord or of Lucifer." (Bruce R. McConkie, in Conference Report, Oct. 1983, p. 106; or *Ensign*, Nov. 1983, p. 73.)

If the book is what it claims to be, if the original record was written on plates of metal and revealed by a holy angel to Joseph Smith, if the translation was made by the power of God, then each of us has the right to know this is true. Consider for a moment the possibility of asking God, the Eternal Father, in the name of his Son, Jesus Christ, if this book is what it is purported to be: "If ye shall ask with a sincere heart, with real intent, having faith in Christ, he will manifest the truth of it unto you, by the power of the Holy Ghost. And by the power of the Holy Ghost ye may know the truth of all things." (Moroni 10:4–5.) Then you will know that the Book of Mormon is the word of God. The Lord himself testified that this was so. (D&C 20:8–10.) The ancient American prophets wrote that this was so. (2 Nephi 33:10; Moroni 7:35.) The translator knew it to be true. (Articles of Faith 1:8.) President Ezra Taft Benson stated that millions of witnesses have known by personal revelation that it is true. (In Conference Report, Oct. 1984, p. 6; or *Ensign*, Nov. 1984, p. 6.)

In humility I include my sincere testimony with the great leaders of this dispensation. I have read and studied the Book of Mormon; I have pondered, prayed, and fasted concerning it. I have sought since my youth to know of its contents. Day after day I have searched as an earnest inquirer after truth.

I have found truth! I have discovered my greatest find, truly my pearl of great price. It is that the Book of Mormon writers wrote primarily about my Savior. They wrote of him because of their conviction of his divinity, for they knew him. Through their obedient efforts I now know of him. Gratitude fills my being for these righteous scribes and for a faithful translator of the word of God. I testify that the Book of Mormon is a powerful, profound witness that Jesus is the Christ, the Son of an Eternal God.

BIBLIOGRAPHY

Anderson, Lavina Fielding. "Kirtland's Resolute Saints," *Ensign*, Jan. 1979, p. 49.

Barrett, Ivan J. *Joseph Smith and the Restoration*. Rev. ed. Provo: Brigham Young University Press, 1973.

Benson, Ezra Taft. In Conference Report, Oct. 1984, pp. 4–7; or *Ensign*, Nov. 1984, pp. 6–8.

————. In Conference Report, Oct. 1986, pp. 3–7; or *Ensign*, Nov. 1986, pp. 4–7.

Cowley, Matthias F. *Wilford Woodruff: History of His Life and Labors*. Salt Lake City: The Deseret News, 1909.

Crandall, Lee A. *New Testament Study on the Use of the Names of Deity*. Mesa, Ariz.: n.p., 1985.

Hymns of The Church of Jesus Christ of Latter-day Saints. Salt Lake City: The Church of Jesus Christ of Latter-day Saints, 1985.

Journal of Discourses. 26 vols. London: Latter-day Saints' Book Depot, 1854–86.

Kimball, Spencer W. In *Improvement Era*, June 1963, pp. 490–95.

Lee, Harold B. *Ye Are the Light of the World: Selected Sermons and Writings of President Harold B. Lee*. Salt Lake City: Deseret Book Co., 1974.

McConkie, Bruce R. *Mormon Doctrine*. 2d ed. Salt Lake City: Bookcraft, 1966.

————. *The Promised Messiah*. Salt Lake City: Deseret Book Co., 1978.

————. In Conference Report, Oct. 1983, pp. 103–7; or *Ensign*, Nov. 1983, pp. 72–74.

Pratt, Parley P. *Autobiography of Parley Parker Pratt*. Salt Lake City: Deseret Book Co., 1980.

Roberts, B. H. *A Comprehensive History of The Church of Jesus Christ of Latter-day Saints*. 6 vols. Provo: The Church of Jesus Christ of Latter-day Saints, 1965.

Smith, George Albert. In Conference Report, Apr. 1936, pp. 13–16.

Smith, Hyrum M., and Sjodahl, Janne E. *The Doctrine and Covenants Commentary.* Rev. ed. Salt Lake City: Deseret Book Co., 1972.

Smith, Joseph. *History of the Church of Jesus Christ of Latter-day Saints.* 7 vols. 2d rev. ed. Ed. B. H. Roberts. Salt Lake City: The Church of Jesus Christ of Latter-day Saints, 1932–51.

Smith, Joseph. *Teachings of the Prophet Joseph Smith.* Sel. Joseph Fielding Smith. Salt Lake City: Deseret Book Co., 1938.

Smith, Joseph Fielding. In *Improvement Era*, Dec. 1961, pp. 924–27.

Talmage, James E. *Jesus the Christ.* 3d ed. Salt Lake City: The Church of Jesus Christ of Latter-day Saints, 1916.

INDEX